Praises for *Civil Society and Citizenship in India and Bangladesh*

This is a fine and thought-provoking collection of articles about civil society in India and Bangladesh—two countries where issues of civil society and those of class, gender, religion and ethnicity (as well as caste) have been historically so intertwined. The articles provide detailed analysis of their case studies, the results of which are useful for comparative analysis and incursions into theoretical debates. Sometimes, work on civil society can appear to be stale, because the concept can mean different things to different people, but in ways often left unacknowledged. The sort of critical awareness necessary to actually enrich discussions of civil society, rather than contribute to its elusiveness, pervades through the book.

—Professor Vedi R. Hadiz

Asia Institute, University of Melbourne, Australia

With civil society 'criticality' under mounting pressure around the world, this excellent and carefully curated collection of essays focusing on gender issues and the status of religious minorities introduces readers to the dynamics shaping the complex relationship between CSOs and the state in today's India and Bangladesh.

—Professor Sarah Ansari

Royal Holloway, University of London

This volume prioritises Tocquevillian associational forms in various actors' engagements in the civil society space. Issues of gender rights, minority rights and state–civil society relations are examined on the basis of painstaking fieldwork in a comparative framework between India and Bangladesh. This volume should be a compulsory read for everyone who is interested in contemporary contests in the civil society space in South Asia, wherein new associational forms are emerging, leading to construction of new parameters of engaged citizenship.

—*Professor Amit Prakash*
Centre for the Study of Law and Governance,
Jawaharlal Nehru University, New Delhi

This edited anthology is a timely and an important contribution to the scholarship on civil society and citizenship, particularly in South Asia. Both empirically and theoretically, this volume meticulously presents the tension and trajectories of relationship between state, civil society and citizenship through exploring women organisations, religion, gender, minority and refugee issues in India and Bangladesh.

—*Associate Professor Mohammad Salehin*
Centre for Peace Studies,
The Arctic University of Norway, Norway

Civil Society and Citizenship in India and Bangladesh

Civil Society and Citizenship in India and Bangladesh

Edited by
Sarbeswar Sahoo and Paul Chaney

B L O O M S B U R Y
NEW DELHI • LONDON • OXFORD • NEW YORK • SYDNEY

BLOOMSBURY INDIA
Bloomsbury Publishing India Pvt. Ltd
Second Floor, LSC Building No. 4, DDA Complex, Pocket C – 6 & 7,
Vasant Kunj, New Delhi, 110070

BLOOMSBURY, BLOOMSBURY ACADEMIC INDIA and the Diana logo
are trademarks of Bloomsbury Publishing Plc

First published in India 2021
This edition published 2021

Bloomsbury Academic
An imprint of Bloomsbury Publishing Plc

ISBN: HB: 978-93-89611-35-9; eBook: 978-93-89611-37-3
2 4 6 8 10 9 7 5 3 1

Typeset in Manipal Technologies Limited
Printed and bound in India by Replika Press Pvt. Ltd.

Contents

Foreword

Civil Society: Some Reflections

Neera Chandhoke

A historian of ideas will testify that concepts that, otherwise, share common vocabularies develop in different ways in discrete historical contexts. Take the concept of civil society. Emerging as a dominant concept in the 1980s in the erstwhile socialist world of Eastern Europe, civil society signified a space where social movements and associations could make demands upon the state, monitor and hold a democratic state accountable, and protest against policies, programmes and laws that were manifestly unjust. Civil society fulfilled a basic proposition of democracy. Ordinary citizens possess the political competence to critique government policies, protest against the oppression of vulnerable groups and propose alternative policies to neutralise injustice. That is why civil society is best thought of as a project of many projects. Some projects affirm each other, some oppose others, some take on the state and others support the state as the condensate of power. There is no one essence to civil society; it is the theatre of democracy.

In the world of the colonised, civil society was not born out of the same historical experience as Europe: an autonomous market, alienation, a juridical order, the individual as the bearer of legal rights and property relations. Civil society organisations in undivided India were related to the freedom struggle and its agenda of social reform, nationalism, uplift of weaker sections, education, charity and welfarism. Nationalism gave rise to the idea that we have obligations to our fellow beings.

This sentiment was subverted by the partition of India in August 1947. The Partition bore dreadful consequences in the shape of involuntary mass migrations, ethnic cleansing, gang rapes and sordid mutilations—all of which have left vivid scars upon the memories of populations on both sides of the border. In 1971, when East Pakistan declared itself independent of Pakistan, an estimated 3 million people died in the war between the new state of Bangladesh and the parent country. About 8 to 10 million were rendered homeless. In another historical context, A.E. Housman had written: 'They say my verse is sad: no wonder, Its narrow measure spans, Tears of eternity and sorrow, Not mine, but man's.' These lines may well provide the epigraph of partitions.

The birth of first two, and three nations was embedded in massive violence. This is the first factor that adversely impacted the body politic in India and Bangladesh. The second factor was the logical consequence of partitions—the minority issue. The third troublesome factor was the emergence of identity politics as a dominant feature of the political scene. And the fourth factor was state-sponsored construction of the nation.

The historian, Hans Kohn, writing in the aftermath of the Second World War had pointed out that territorially based civic nationalism is qualitatively distinct from cultural or ethnic nationalism. The former, which developed in England, the United States and France, represented predominantly a political movement to limit governmental power, and to secure civic rights. The temporal and the spatial contexts for ethnic nationalism, which arose later in Central and Eastern Europe and in Asia, were different. Consolidated amidst social and economic underdevelopment, and emerging in direct opposition to state power, ethnic nationalism was first articulated in the aesthetic and cultural field. Kohn's distinction between civic and ethnic nationalism set the stage for much of the subsequent discussion on the subject.

In undivided India and then in Bangladesh, the shape that nationalism took was dramatically different. Civic and ethnic nationalism based on identity came up at the same time, and intertwined in different ways. In the biography of both countries, civic nationalism has never been entirely free of anxieties about identity, and very soon political elites came to rely on religion/language to legitimise their rule. Not surprisingly, major parts of civil society in both countries were split along the axis of religion/language and majoritarianism. Democratic civil society organisations had to deal with states that drew upon majoritarian identities to support their rule, and societies that backed the project. Consequently, civil society in both India and Bangladesh have had to be Janus-faced, with one face directed towards the state and the other towards the society. That is, civil society organisations have not only taken on the task of monitoring increasingly repressive states and holding them accountable, but also representing and struggling for the rights of women, religious/ethnic minorities and other vulnerable sections, and countering religious authoritarianism and communal violence. Civil society is burdened with many more tasks than its counterpart in the Western world. To complicate the issue, consider some of the problems confronted by civil society organisations.

The editors of this volume, Sarbeswar Sahoo and Paul Chaney, point out that various news reports and international commissions have registered the rise of majoritarianism in Bangladesh and India. Governments have not only failed to protect minorities, they have often colluded with and even crafted majoritarian agendas. They have thus violated constitutional rights guaranteed to minorities. Communal riots have had terrible side effects. The Urdu poet Saghar Khayyami (2008) writes of the way leaders of the latter variant have corrupted religion: '*Aisi koi missal zamaane ne paayi ho/Hindu ke ghar mein aag khuda ne lagaayi ho/Basti kisi ki Ram ne yaaro jaalayi ho/Nanak ne sirf raah sikhon ko dikhayi ho/ Ram-Raheem-o-Nanak-o/ Eesha toh narm hai/chamchon ko dekhiye toh pateeli se garm hai*' (Saif Mahmood, 2016). Can anyone, asks the poet, give an example where God set fire to Hindu homes? Has anyone witnessed Lord Ram burning a settlement? Can anyone believe that Nanak showed the right path only to Sikhs? Ram, Raheem, Nanak and Eesa are gentle, but their courtiers are constantly on the boil. They burn more than a scorching pot.

The struggle in Bangladesh and India for citizenship rights has taken a hard knock with governments cracking down on human rights organisations. Naturally, repressive governments have no problem with service delivery organisations. But they have no time for social movements or for civil society activists. Sahoo notes that, in recent years, the state has become rigid and overbearing in India. In both states, the space for civil society activism has shrunk dramatically.

Admittedly, the relationship between the state and civil society is complex and even contradictory. Chaney discusses in some details how Bangladesh has tackled the migration of Rohingyas fleeing persecution in Myanmar. Civil society organisations have defended the rights of migrants to citizenship although the government is less than enthusiastic. But they are also conscious of the limits on state policy. Civil society does not confront the state in every case. Yet, even as the states reinforce their power, they move relentlessly to stifle civil society.

There was a time when South Asians believed that civil and political rights had been secured by constitutions and by civil liberty organisations, and we could move onto secure social rights. Today, we find that we have to begin the struggle for civil and political rights of citizenship anew. The celebrated argument of T.H. Marshall—that rights come in stages—does not hold in our part of the world. We have to think of rights as a package that has to be renewed periodically. Civil society has to shoulder another task, that of rethinking the idea of rights.

Repression of civil society activism has had a deleterious effect on gender equality in both the states. India and Bangladesh's historical record of gender equality is poor. One may suggest that civil society organisations should concentrate on policy-making and ensure that policies deal with women's rights. Yet, in a patriarchal world, the efficacy of this strategy is debatable, considering that women's representation in all political institutions has declined rapidly. Moreover, feminist movements in civil society are split on the issue of women's agency, and on the strategy to be employed in fighting patriarchy as Rajeshwari points out. Seuty Sabur focuses on the same problem in the case of Bangladesh. Finally, the issue of fragmentation and the bureaucratisation of civil society organisations is no doubt a problematic one. Islam and Sarkar conclude that the relationship between the state and civil society is ridden with ambivalences in Bangladesh. The case of India is not much better.

Yet, there are certain givens. Civil society enables citizens to come together in all manners of projects to monitor centres of power. We must, however, keep in mind the following fact. Whereas a democratic civil society is an indispensable precondition of a democratic state. a democratic state is also a necessary precondition for civil society. When states turn authoritarian, what the fate of civil society will be is an open question. Civil society is a fragmented space, with some organisations participating in projects of state power and others resisting these projects. Civil society is messy, chaotic and noisy. But it can also be creative. The proviso is that democratic associations in civil society are prepared to take on both, the state as well as other institutions in society, from the patriarchal family to the patriarchal state, from a state obsessed with power to a market obsessed with profit. Finally, civil society gives us no solutions to political predicaments. But the concept provides both the space and the values for people to come together in solidarity. States with civil societies may not be entirely democratic. But states without civil societies cannot claim democracy at all.

Reference

Mahmood, Saif. 2016. 'The Secular Agenda of Humorist Urdu Poetry'. Available at https://www.sabrangindia.in/column/secular-agenda-humourist-urdu-poetry (accessed on 18 June 2019).

Acknowledgements

We gratefully acknowledge grants funding from the Academy of Medical Sciences, Global Challenge Research Fund, Award No. GCRFNG100259 and the Economic and Social Research Council, Award No. ES/S012435/1. These grants enabled us to conduct fieldwork for our respective chapters and organise workshops at which these papers were presented and discussed.

We also acknowledge the administrative and intellectual support we received during the project period from the Department of Humanities and Social Sciences (IIT Delhi, India), the Department of Economics and Social Sciences (BRAC University, Bangladesh) and Wales Institute of Social and Economic Research, Data and Methods (WISERD, Cardiff University, Wales, UK).

Finally, we would like to thank R. Chandra Sekhar at Bloomsbury Publishing for his interest in this project and for his cooperation and support during the publication of this book.

Introduction

Sarbeswar Sahoo and Paul Chaney

This book explores the relationship between civil society and citizenship rights in India and Bangladesh. It brings together case studies on three important areas: gender rights, minority rights and state–civil society relations. The 75th anniversary of the Universal Declaration of Human Rights is an appropriate juncture to take stock of these issues in relation to citizenship in both the countries. Not least because, at their founding in 1947 and 1971, their constitutions aspired to new citizenship practices founded on notions of rights, equality and democracy. The 25th anniversary of the Beijing Declaration of 1995 also underlines the timeliness of an assessment of gender rights.

Historically, South Asia has a poor record of sex discrimination and gender oppression (Ansari and Gould, 2019). For its part, the United Nations observed that:

> Although India's Constitution had been one of the first to embody the principle of women's equality, the Government's policy of non-interference in the personal affairs of any community without its initiative and consent tended to perpetuate traditional forms of discrimination against women. The power of the religious communities to determine the civil status laws that governed their members resulted in inequality before the law not only between women and men but also between the women of different communities. (UN, CEDAW, 2000)

Moreover, the Committee on the Elimination of Discrimination against Women underlined that: 'Laws punishing violence against women were clearly not enough. There [is...] an urgent need for public education programmes to make the general public recognize that such violence [... is] completely unacceptable'

(UN, CEDAW, 2000). Furthermore, analysis of labour market practices reveal: 'Women are more likely than men to experience insecure employment; a gender pay gap is widespread; [and] horizontal segregation by gender abounds with women occupying a narrower range of occupations than men which frequently reflect women's accepted social roles of nurturer' (Strachan, Adikaram and Kailasapathy, 2015). Country studies also underline how 'state-driven policy delivery … undermines the capacity of the civil sphere to challenge the traditionally male-dominated power structures and hampers progress towards the normative vision of gender equality set out in UN policy' (Chaney, 2015).

Studies of minority rights in the two countries also reveal widespread marginalisation, intolerance, incitement, forced conversion and communal violence (Sahoo, 2013, 2018; Chaney, 2019; Chaney and Sahoo, 2020). The United States Commission on International Religious Freedom (USCIRF) has expressed grave concerns over declining religious freedom in these two countries. In case of Bangladesh, the USCIRF noted that forced conversion of young children belonging to indigenous groups to Islam, and forced conversion and marriage of minority women to Muslim men have seriously undermined the religious freedom rights of minorities and indigenous populations (USCIRF, 2018). Similarly, in India, it noted that in 2019, religious freedom conditions have experienced a drastic turn downward; therefore, the Commission downgraded India to its lowest ranking 'Countries of Particular Concern (CPC)' (USCIRF, 2020). In response, the Indian government has rejected the observations of USCIRF and has described it as an 'Organization of Particular Concern (OPC)'.

Notwithstanding this, what the USCIRF and several news reports show is that the various governments and political regimes in India and Bangladesh have not only failed to protect but have also often colluded with the majorities in undermining the constitutional rights of the minorities. Such processes can be seen as part of a wider international trend whereby identity politics are challenging contemporary patterns and processes of governance as they seek to address social cleavages related to class and protected characteristics and end discrimination, oppression and inequality (Chaney, 2021).

Moreover, in terms of state–civil society relations, the civil sphere has long suffered periods of state oppression, restricting citizens' rights and freedoms. For example, writing of Bangladesh almost three decades ago Rizvi (1994) referred to how 'repeated military interventions and prolonged periods of authoritarian rule [… have] undermined democratic institutions, systematically deinstitutionalised the various governmental and constitutional organs and emaciated the institutions of civil society'. In a similar vein, more recent analysis has alluded to how 'the country continues to confront major challenges of fostering a culture of democracy, human rights and the rule of law, as the politics of mutual mistrust has re-emerged with renewed strengths into Bangladesh's rather dysfunctional political landscape' (Hudson, Fahimul and Yutaka, 2015). The result is 'on-going rights violations in an increasingly hostile political context wherein government is unresponsive to civil society claims, mobilization is suppressed and CSOs are forced to focus on service delivery and advocacy functions' (Chaney, 2017). In the case of India, there are also concerns over restrictions on civic and democratic space (see Behar, 2019). Thus, from an international perspective, contemporary scholarship notes the ongoing challenges that civil society organisations (CSOs) face in both liberal democracies and more authoritarian contexts (Chaney, 2018a, 2018b, 2019).

Varying Conceptions of Civil Society and Citizenship

Given the above backdrop, it is useful to discuss the two fundamental concepts used in this book: civil society and citizenship. The basic questions are: how do we understand civil society and what is its nature in India and Bangladesh? How is citizenship understood in these two different political contexts? And, in what ways does civil society contribute to the strengthening of citizenship rights? In this book, we argue that civil society is not a monolithic concept. Conceptions of civil society vary widely (Sahoo, 2013; Jensen, 2006).[1] While some scholars have defined civil society as the sphere of 'associational life' (De Tocqueville, 1835), others have described it as the intermediate 'third sphere' between state and market (Chandhoke, 2001; Cohen and Arato, 1992). Such differentiation and autonomy of civil society from the state first appeared in the modernist conception of civil society where political theorists defined it as a domain parallel to, but separate from, the state (see Sahoo, 2013).

One of the early modern theorists of civil society was Georg Hegel who defined civil society 'as the domain of particularity between the patriarchal family and the universal state—the totality of material conditions of life' (Sahoo, 2013). While Hegel noted that the state and civil society are two distinct and autonomous domains, he was of the opinion that it is the state which has the power to intervene in civil society to control its disruptive tendencies for the larger common interests of society (Sahoo, 2013). In striking contrast to Hegel, Marx subordinated the state to civil society and argued that 'civil society is the true source and theatre of all history' (Comaroff and Comaroff, 1999). Neo-Marxist scholars like Gramsci, however, provided a much more nuanced understanding of the relationship between state and civil society. In contra-distinction to Hegel and Marx, who defined civil society as a domain of economic needs, Gramsci saw it as predominantly a political site—a site of both hegemonic and counter-hegemonic struggle (see Kumar, 1993). On the one hand, forces within civil society may collaborate with the state and help advance capitalistic state hegemony; on the other hand, civil society can also mobilise against the state to make it more accountable and democratic. Furthermore, other scholars such as Habermas defined civil society as the 'public sphere' where private individuals transcend their ascribed identities and come together as a public and form an interactive body of citizens engaged in a rational critical discourse (Calhoun, 1992; Sahoo, 2006).

In this volume, we follow the liberal De Tocquevillian view of civil society as non-state associational sphere. According to this, civil society is neither governed by the logic of acquiring state power (like political parties) nor by the logic of maximising profit (as with private enterprises following market forces). Instead, civil society's objective is to act as a 'sphere of solidarity' (Alexander, 1997) and protect public interest and democratic values. This begs the question: Does civil society always protect and promote public interests and democratic values? In this volume, we argue that the intermediate sphere of civil associational life is inherently heterogeneous in nature. There are civil as well as uncivil, legal as well as illegal and political as well as apolitical forces that operate within this sphere. Given the prevalence of such plurality of forces, it is difficult to draw a direct and straightforward relationship between civil society and democracy. In fact, there might be some *uncivil* forces, which instead of promoting may even undermine democracy. This shows that civil society's contribution to democratic development is contingent upon the kinds of forces that are dominant within the domain of civil society (Sahoo, 2013; Chaney, 2016).

Notwithstanding the fact that a fraction of civil society may undermine democracy, it is undeniable that a large majority of CSOs have been playing a vital role in advancing the democratic project. Specifically, in liberal democracies, when the state tries to violate or undermine democratic values, civil society mobilises to resist such hegemonic tendencies and make the state accountable to the public. Crucially, thus, for De Tocqueville, a strong, vibrant arena of civil associational life acts as the watchdog of democracy and upholds citizenship rights. Recognising such a role, the United Nations Office of the High Commissioner for Human Rights provides a strong reminder of the value of a strong and vibrant civil society:

> Participation in public life by rights holders and organizations that represent them is a fundamental principle of human rights. Participation also improves the efficacy of political systems, as well as policy development and implementation. Civil society space is therefore a threshold issue, not only for human rights, but also for development and peace and security more broadly. When civil society sits at the table, policy-making is more informed, effective and sustainable. Each advance in protecting civic space has a positive ripple effect for communities and individuals and their rights. (OHCHR, 2018)

However, as some of the chapters in this volume reveal, under centralised and authoritarian governing practices, civil society is often oppressed and the state ignores its commitments to democratic values and citizenship rights (see Lewis, 2013).

Our second concept, citizenship, becomes very relevant here. According to the British sociologist, T.H. Marshall (1950), 'Citizenship is a status bestowed on those who are full members of a community'. For him, 'All who possess the status are equal with respect to the rights and duties with which the status is endowed'. One of the key elements determining one's citizenship is the membership of a political community or 'legal status' of an individual within the nation-state. Because of this integral relationship, some scholars have referred to citizenship as 'nationalised citizenship', i.e., '[o]nly nation-states have citizens and only nation-states may grant citizenship' (see Klug, 2000).

According to this notion of nationalised citizenship, 'birth' within a nation-state becomes an important factor of citizenship. Yet, as Klug (2000) argues, 'Birth-right does not guarantee political or other rights, let alone the promise of identity, solidarity, and participation inherent in more deeply textured notion of citizenship'. Furthermore, the prevalence of 'refugee status'—a form of legal statelessness as seen in the case of the Rohingya people in Bangladesh (see Chapter 3)—also complicates the notion of nationalised citizenship. Given these limitations, and taking into account the contextual and transnational character of our current existence, several scholars have advocated for 'contextual'/'denationalized citizenship' (Klug, 2000) or 'flexible citizenship' (Ong, 1999).[2]

According to Turner (2017), there are four modes or 'ideal types' of citizenship. The first is national citizenship. This is integral to ethno-nationalism and nation-building. The second is social citizenship. This emphasises civil society institutions and is concerned with social rights and the provision of social welfare. The latter refers to collective, interventionist measures concerned with how we look after each other as human beings. Traditionally, it is linked to basic public goods such as health care, housing, education and social services. For this reason, it is sometimes dubbed as 'welfare citizenship' (Chaney, 2017b). The third form is concerned with participation in the labour market, and notions of self-reliance and autonomy. And, the fourth model of citizenship 'presupposes a consumer society, a weak state and the decline of civic institutions' (p. 11). Discussing these four different ideal types, Turner (2017) suggests that rather than viewing these modes of citizenship as discrete, multiple hybridised forms may instead prevail.

Through these different notions, Klug (2000), Ong (1999) and Turner (2017) seek to advance contextualised, pluri-dimensional notions of citizenship. To them, meanings of and struggles around citizenship are contingent upon cultural, economic and social contexts. As Ong (1999) argues, citizenship is not a legal-political right tied to the participation/loyalty of the members to the nation-state; instead, it is an idea that is governed by the cultural and economic logics of globalisation and transnationalism. To her, in the age of globalisation, people chose their citizenship based on economic reasons rather than legal-political rights or participation within whichever nation-state they reside. The citizenship literature is thus moving away from the nationalised/legal status notions of citizenship and is providing a multidimensional understanding, especially emphasising the social, cultural and economic rights.

One of the early scholars who discussed the social and economic aspects of citizenship was T.H. Marshall. Besides membership (civil/legal citizenship), Marshall (1950) also advanced political citizenship (universal suffrage) and social/welfare citizenship (state ensuring members a basic level of social and cultural well-being).[3] In the postcolonial political context, especially in India and Bangladesh, although a vast majority of people enjoy civil/formal citizenship by being members of the nation-state, they lack substantive citizenship; they are deprived of exercising their fundamental rights and the state has failed to provide a basic level of social welfare and security to them. As Holston and Appadurai (1996) argue:

> Formal membership in the nation-state is increasingly neither a necessary nor a sufficient condition for substantive citizenship. That it is not sufficient is obvious for many poor citizens who have formal membership in the state but who are excluded in fact or law from enjoying the rights of citizenship and participating effectively in its organization.

Niraja Jayal (2013) has, therefore, emphasised the need to ensure people's social and economic rights and has argued that they are central to achieving substantive citizenship. She notes that:

> Equality is the premise of citizenship, but equal civil and political rights in and of themselves are poor guarantors of substantive equality, their egalitarian promise constantly undermined by the social inequalities that obtain in society. Social and economic rights are widely acknowledged as the principal means by which citizenship's promise of equality and the difficulty of its attainment may be mediated. (Jayal, 2013)

However, the failure of the state to reach out to the people at the margins, as well as its recent withdrawal owing to the policies of neoliberalism, has made it difficult to achieve substantive citizenship for a vast majority of people in many postcolonial contexts. This is particularly evident in India and Bangladesh, as a significant percentage of their population live under the poverty line, lack basic education and health care and are unable to exercise the fundamental rights enshrined in their constitutions. Strikingly, Turner (2017) argues that:

> … [Under] economic globalisation and the development of neoliberal strategies, the various forms of citizenship have converged towards a new model of passive citizenship in which the state is or has withdrawn from commitment to full employment and the provision of social security, especially universal provision of welfare services, and civil society institutions have been eroded. The market rather than civil society has become the institutional setting for citizenship.

The withdrawal of the (welfare) state on the one hand, as well as the dominance of the market and the neoliberal restructuring of the economy on the other, have adversely affected the socioeconomic rights and interests of the poor and marginalised groups. It has also led to various displacements and dislocations in their lives. In this context, as Polanyi (2001 [1944]) had argued, and as Sahoo (2017) shows in the case of India, the unregulated expansion of the market gives rise to several reactionary political movements in the domain of civil society.[4] The objective of these civil society movements is to socially embed the market, make economic growth humane and inclusive and advance and protect the interests and welfare rights of the vulnerable groups. As Chandhoke (2013) has rightly argued, in the context of 'crisis of representation', where the state and political parties have failed to represent the interests of people, it is the CSOs that have advanced the project of empowerment, citizenship rights and good governance. She notes in the context of India that:

> Indisputably, civil society groups have succeeded in … bringing to the forefront of social attention issues of poverty, marginality, and deprivation, urged the government to enact social policy to neutralise ill-being, and focussed on violation of human rights. Though we cannot say that India is in the throes of a social revolution, in a

> substantial sense, NGOs have tried to *realise* democracy by focussing attention on issues that have been left untouched by political representatives, whether the issue of civil liberties, or communalism, or right to food, or the right to work, or the right to information. (Chandhoke, 2013)[5]

This shows that NGOs and CSOs have played a substantial role in *representing*[6] the rights and interests of the marginalised communities. Specifically, as data suggests, there are more than 3.2 million CSOs in India (Chapter 4) and 1,132 in Bangladesh (Chapter 5) that have been working to improve the socioeconomic conditions of many vulnerable and marginal groups. Considering this, the book thus attempts to understand the roles that CSOs and movements play in advancing citizenship rights, not only in the legal sense of the term but also in the social sense, especially in regard to the socioeconomic and political rights of women, minorities and other marginalised groups.

Situating the Contributions

Having contextualised the current area of enquiry with reference to foundational concepts, we now discuss some central questions and the structure of the remainder of this volume. Besides introduction and conclusion, this volume has five chapters. Each engages empirically and theoretically with the concepts of civil society and citizenship and the relationship between the two and shows the ways in which CSOs either advance or obstruct citizenship in relation to women, minorities and other marginalised groups.

Civil Society and Gender Rights

As mentioned earlier, South Asia in general and India and Bangladesh in particular have a poor record of gender equality. Both countries have been subject to 'longstanding historical patterns and process of gender-based discrimination and oppression' (Chaney, 2015). Women in these countries suffer from various biases and discriminations. Despite various constitutional provisions that prohibit any kind of discrimination on the basis of sex/gender, women are treated unequally not just within the household but also in the public domain. Women's political representation and work participation rates are extremely low. Furthermore, these two countries have performed miserably in the United Nation's Gender Development Index (GDI) and Gender Inequality Index (GII).[7]

Given this, the question is, how to improve the condition of women and protect and promote their basic human rights. In regard to the state, it is observed that power structures have traditionally remained male-dominated, which has hampered the goal of achieving gender equality. Given this, Chaney (2015) argues that CSOs can play a major role in 'mainstreaming' gender within the state, specifically by '[embedding] gender equality concerns in every stage of the policy process'. Furthermore, he argues that CSOs can also 'advocate, politicise and provide services for women through representation and gendered claims-making cognizant of a history of marginalization and oppression' (p. 380).

Thus, in the first two chapters (Chapters 1 and 2), we examine the complexities and challenges surrounding women's rights and the role that civil society, especially women's organisations and movements, play in addressing them. In these chapters, we ask: what is the nature of women's organisations and movements in India and Bangladesh? How do these organisations and movements contribute to democratic development and nation-building in general and the advancement of women's rights in particular? Do all kinds of women's organisations and movements help build women's agency and advance gender inclusive citizenship rights? Drawing on historical and contemporary case studies and narratives, the two chapters argue that while women's movements and organisations have historically played a significant role in building women's agency and representing their rights and interests in the public/political sphere, at present, they have increasingly been depoliticised and fragmented.

Addressing aspects of such fragmentation of the women's movement in India, in Chapter 1, B. Rajeshwari discusses the various ways in which the patriarchal and fundamentalist forces have misappropriated aspects of the women's question, which has posed severe threats to equality and gender inclusive citizenship rights. Furthermore, discussing several other aspects of gender fragmentation, especially the controversies and contradictions surrounding personal laws and women's temple-entry question, Rajeshwari argues that, while on the one hand, feminists and feminist women's movements claim to be representing women's rights, on the other hand, several women and women's groups have claimed that such movements have undermined ordinary women's agency and misrepresented their issues. Given these existing fragmentations, Rajeshwari argues that the challenge before the feminist civil society groups is to recognise the growing agency of alternate women's voices that are moving away from liberal/individualistic interpretation of women's citizenship.

In Chapter 2, Seuty Sabur also discusses aspects of this fragmentation and depoliticisation of the women's movement in Bangladesh. According to her, while in the early period women's organisations acted as an effective *political* force in advancing women's rights and contributing to nation-building process, many of them eventually lost their political character in the 1980s with the neoliberal turn and became heavily bureaucratised, NGO-ised and depoliticised. Moreover, several of the social movements, including women's movements that had emerged organically over the years, got co-opted within the state-donor nexus. Given this, the question is how has the political field in Bangladesh changed and in what ways do women's rights activists and organisations advance gender inclusive citizenship rights? Drawing from the women's organisations' literature, oral histories and interviews, Sabur documents the experiences and contributions of women's rights activists in the last few decades and shows how each generation of women's rights activists were uniquely positioned with different imaginations of citizenship and 'the nation'. In particular, Sabur highlights the everyday politics that have shaped what feminism looks like, as well as the subjects that are embedded within such a complex field.

Civil Society and Minorities

By minorities, we refer to all those individuals and groups whose access to socioeconomic and political processes and institutions is limited primarily because of their identities, such as caste, ethnicity, religion or gender. Democracies are often judged on the way they treat their minorities. In the South Asian context, minorities have historically been discriminated against. Specifically, in India, ethnic minorities like the Dalits and Adivasis have traditionally been oppressed by mainstream society and upper-caste groups (see Prakash, 2001). Furthermore, as Varshney (2002) has noted, Hindu–Muslim communalism has been the 'master narrative' of postcolonial India. Since 1990s, there has also been rising 'Christianophobia' and violence against Christians has increased significantly (Sahoo, 2018). Moreover, minority representation in public and political life is very limited. The Sachar Committee Report had long ago highlighted the extreme underrepresentation of Muslims in Indian public life.[8] A recent study by Farah Naqvi and the Sadbhavna Trust (2018) has also highlighted the various vulnerabilities and developmental deficits that Muslim citizens face in India.

Similarly, in the Bangladesh, the Hindus and other ethnic and religious minority groups have been severely harassed by conservative Islamic groups.[9] As discussed above, indigenous people and minorities are sometimes forced to convert to Islam and minority women are forced to not only convert, but also marry Muslim men; minority properties are also often forcibly taken away. Besides, the 15th Amendment to the Bangladesh Constitution that confirmed

Islam as the state religion has not only undermined secularism, but also escalated attacks and threats against religious minorities and further deteriorated their situation (Chaney and Sahoo, 2020).

Despite various constitutional provisions, minorities of India and Bangladesh are deprived of their basic citizenship rights. This is because, as Prakash (2001) argues, majoritarian ethnic groups not only seek to have a 'major say in the political system in order to protect, preserve and promote their interests', but also '[aspire] for a national status and/or political recognition either within an existing State or as a new State'. In such contexts, minorities have experienced 'uneven/hierarchical citizenship' and have lived like 'second-class citizens'.[10] The situation has worsened when the state began siding with the majorities and actively pursued their agenda of nationalism. The state, instead of protecting minority rights, deliberately ignored its commitments to constitutional and democratic values. The question one may then ask is when the state acts in a majoritarian way and ignores its commitments, who is going to protect and advocate for the minority rights? In this context, CSOs have played a major role, not just in advocating for the freedoms and citizenship rights of minorities, but also in defending religious pluralism while also reminding the state its constitutional obligations. As Aiyar and Malik (2004) note:

> Civil society, despite its limitations, is an important space within which marginalised communities can articulate their needs and demands and negotiate with the state for their rights. In the current context in India [though it was written in 2004, it remains relevant in 2020 as well], where Muslims have been marginalised in the political sphere the role that civil society can play in providing the necessary space for Muslims to articulate their needs is particularly relevant.

In Chapter 3, Paul Chaney analyses the watchdog role of CSOs in reminding the Bangladeshi state of its obligations towards defending basic human rights, especially of the stateless non-citizens like the Rohingyas. He examines the crisis facing an estimated 900,000

Rohingya people, a Muslim minority group (a variation of the Sunni religion) that have fled persecution in the western state of Rakhine, Myanmar, and have sought sanctuary in the south-eastern district of Cox's Bazar in Bangladesh. Discussing the 'situated knowledge' of CSOs working with the refugees, Chaney reveals how the Bangladeshi state has failed to fulfil its commitments to ensuring basic human rights of the Rohingyas who are subject to a broad range of rights violations: denial of citizenship access to health care, violence, intimidation and sex trafficking. Furthermore, discussing the 'disconnect' between state and civil society in dealing with the crisis, Chaney shows that representational failings to fully engage the Rohingyas in shaping the Bangladesh government's crisis-relief response means that, when formulating the disaster response, political elites and policy-makers need to be cognisant of a myriad of political narratives on the issue; failure to do so may lead to performativity and legitimation instead of legitimacy and efficacy in rights observance.

State and Civil Society Relations

In the last two chapters (Chapters 4 and 5), we discuss what Chaney in Chapter 3 has referred to as the 'disconnect' between the state and the civil society. In order to explain this, it is vital to understand the state-civil society relationship in a *longue durée* approach. The questions are: what is the nature of state and civil society relationship in India and Bangladesh? And, what implications does this relationship have for the autonomy of civil society and state effectiveness on the one hand as well as citizenship rights and democratic development on the other?

As discussed earlier, state and civil society relationships are complex, contingent and dynamic in nature; they are shaped by time, context, nature of the political regime and several other institutional and ideological factors. They are also dependent on the nature of the state as well as the nature of the civil society. According to

Chandhoke (2001), it is the state which acts as the 'enabler of civil society' and 'provides the legal and political settings' for civil society to exist and maintain itself. In other words, 'the state is a *precondition* for the existence of civil society' (p. 8). Given this, the nature of the state/regime and the forces/interests that dominate its sphere heavily determine whether civil society will have the freedom to pursue its transformative agenda.

While authoritarian states severely restrict the autonomy of civil society, democratic states act as facilitators. However, it has been observed that many formal democracies can also be dominated by illiberal and majoritarian forces, which may suppress civil society and prevent it from pursuing democratic agenda. What should the civil society then do? In such contexts, civil society may pursue a counter-hegemonic agenda and force the state to act democratically. This does not mean civil society always behaves in an anti-state manner; it can also cooperate with the state and promote democratic development and citizenship rights. Furthermore, as discussed earlier, civil society does not necessarily always promote democracy. There are uncivil forces within civil society, which may also undermine democratic development (Sahoo, 2013, 2019). This shows that state–civil society relationship is dynamic in nature and may take various forms—being both cooperative and conflictual.

Addressing some aspects of this dynamic relationship, Sahoo (in Chapter 4) discusses the limited scope and functioning of civil society in India today. Taking a long-term perspective, Sahoo argues that restrictions on civil society are not new to India. While state and civil society shared a cooperative relationship during the Nehruvian period, during Indira Gandhi's regime, civil society experienced severe restrictions. After a period of suppression and harassment, Rajiv Gandhi's government partnered with and supported the CSOs. While successive governments have recognised the importance of CSOs in development, they have been very selective. In their attempts to implement neoliberal policies, governments have promoted organisations that follow the apolitical welfare and service delivery approach and restricted severely the CSOs that are political in nature. As a consequence, a large section of civil society in India has been depoliticised.

Similarly, in Chapter 5, Islam and Sarkar discuss the trajectory of state–civil society interaction in Bangladesh. They argue that although CSOs have contributed significantly to the development of Bangladesh, their relationship with the state has not been that smooth or easy-going. According to them, state and civil society relations in Bangladesh could be seen in terms of: (a) cooperation, (b) confrontation and (c) partnership. While, after independence, CSOs were invited to promote development in the war-damaged and poverty-ridden Bangladesh, during the military regime, their autonomy was heavily curtailed. Subsequently, the state has also partnered with CSOs in implementing various development programmes. In this partnership, the bureaucratic approach of the state and flexibility of civil society are expected to act as checks and balances on each other. Thus, Islam and Sarkar show that a critical revisit of the engagement between the state and civil society in Bangladesh unfolds a complex and dynamic relationship, which is not just harmonious but contentious as well.

In 'Conclusions', Chaney and Sahoo highlight some of the major trends and reflect upon the empirical findings presented in this collection and their implications for policy and practice, as well as a social theory.

Collectively, the chapters in this volume critically examine the importance of civil society in advancing the interests and citizenship rights of women, ethnic and religious minorities and other marginalised groups in India and Bangladesh. Particularly, the essays show that despite the fact that the civil society domain is fragmented and a section of it may advance illiberal values, there is little doubt that civil society is also one of the principal agents of democratisation. It not only collaborates with the state in implementing a good governance agenda, it also acts as a watchdog and resists the state when the state becomes unaccountable or undermines public interest and citizenship rights. Broadly, civil society acts as 'the realm of freedom' (Rudolph, 2000); it is an individual's protection against the illiberal state and exploitative market. Without civil societies, democracies would struggle to survive; therefore, protecting the basic autonomy or freedom of civil society is the urgent need of the hour in India and Bangladesh.

Notes

1. While Sahoo (2013) discusses the liberal-pluralist, the neo-Marxist and the Communitarian understandings of civil society, Jensen (2006) discusses the pluralist conceptions of civil society through an analysis of the *sphere concept*, the *Lockean concept* and the *Scottish concept.*
2. Some scholars have also discussed the concept of 'lived citizenship' that is 'the meaning that citizenship actually has in people's lives and the ways in which people's social and cultural backgrounds and material circumstances affect their lives as citizens' (see Lister, 2003, 3).
3. Drawing on the works of T.H. Marshall, Niraja Jayal (2013, 13) has also discussed three forms of citizenship: citizenship as legal status, citizenship as rights and entitlements and citizenship as a form of identity and belonging.
4. Discussing the case of India, Sahoo (2017) has pointed out four different kinds of reactionary or countermovements to market liberalism: (a) reactionary, (b) reformist, (c) welfarist/developmental and (d) political.
5. However, Chandhoke (2013) further argues that although there is no doubt that CSOs have played a vital role in foregrounding social and economic rights of the poor, the question that still remains is: 'how much can the NGO sector achieve? For one, civil society agents are just not in a position to summon up the kind of resources that are required to emancipate citizens from poverty and deprivation'. Considering this, Chandhoke believes that it is only the state that can mobilise resources for people's development.

6. For more on how development organisations represent the poor and marginalised groups and contribute towards inclusive development in India, see Katyaini, Van Wessel and Sahoo (2021).
7. As per the 2018 data, India has scored 0.829 and Bangladesh 0.895 compared to the best HDI performer, Norway, which scored 0.990 (http://hdr.undp.org/en/indicators/137906; last accessed 17 July 2020). Similarly, in GII, India has a score of 0.501 and Bangladesh of 0.536 compared to the best HDI performer, Norway, which has a score of 0.044 (http://hdr.undp.org/en/indicators/68606; last accessed 17 July 2020).
8. Aiyar and Malik (2004) also show how 'the Indian state has failed to recognise and actively address the issue of socio-economic rights of Muslims'.
9. Farzana (2009) has discussed the case of Biharis in Bangladesh and described them as 'artificial minority' who are facing the problem of 'statelessness'. According to her,

   > despite the fact that [the Biharis] are similar to the majority Bengali people in that they share a common religion, Islam, and have come to share a common language, Bangla, in Bangladesh [they] are treated differently in terms of identity, nationality, and social, economic and political status.

10. Gopal Guru's concept of 'exiled citizenship' (2005) may be useful to explain the case of minorities in India and Bangladesh. Just like the Dalits of India, minorities also 'face an almost comprehensive exclusion from the public sphere' in these two countries and, therefore, can be referred to as 'exiled citizens'.

References

Aiyar, Y. and M. Malik. 2004. 'Minority Rights, Secularism and Civil Society'. *Economic and Political Weekly*, 39(43): 4707–4711.

Alexander, J.C. 1997. 'The Paradoxes of Civil Society'. *International Sociology*, 12(2): 115–133.

Ansari, S. and W. Gould. 2019. *Boundaries of Belonging: Localities, Citizenship and Rights in India and Pakistan*. Cambridge: Cambridge University Press.

Behar, A. 2019. 'The Shrinking Civil Society Space: Re-engineering the Architecture of Democratic India'. In *Re-forming India: The Nation Today*, edited by N.G. Jayal, 404–419. New Delhi: Penguin-Viking.

Calhoun, C. (ed.). 1992. *Habermas and the Public Sphere.* Cambridge: The MIT Press.

Chandhoke, N. 2001. 'The "Civil" and "Political" in Civil Society'. *Democratization,* 8(2): 1–24.

_______. 2013. 'The Representation Deficit in Civil Society'. In *Indian Democracy (Volume 2),* edited by K.C. Suri, 253–273. New Delhi: Oxford University Press.

Chaney, P. 2015. 'The "Complementarity Conjecture"—Does Civil Society Engagement Strengthen Input Legitimacy and Shape Policy Delivery? The Case of Gender Mainstreaming in India and Nepal 2005–15'. *Journal of Comparative Asian Development*, 14(3): 377–413.

________. 2016. 'Gendered Political Space: Civil Society, Contingency Theory and the Substantive Representation of Women'. *Journal of Civil Society*, 12(2): 198–223.

________. 2017a. 'Limited Gains, Enduring Violations: Civil Society Perspectives on the Implementation of the United Nations' Convention on the Rights of the Child in Bangladesh'. *Journal of South Asian Development*, 12(3): 1–22.

________. 2017b. 'Comparative Analysis of Civil Society and State Discourse on Disabled People's Rights and Welfare in South Asia 2010–16'. *Asian Studies Review*, 41(3): 36–51.

________. 2018a. 'Civil Society, Human Rights and Religious Freedom in the People's Republic of China: Analysis of CSOs' Universal Periodic Review Discourse'. *International Journal of Human Rights*, 22(4): 503–524.

________. 2018b. 'Civil Society, "Traditional Values" and LGBT Resistance to Heteronormative Rights Hegemony: Analysis of the UN Universal Periodic Review in the Russian Federation'. *Europe-Asia Studies*, 70(4): 638–665.

________. 2019. 'India at the Crossroads? Civil Society, Human Rights and Religious Freedom: Critical Analysis of CSOs' Third Cycle Universal Periodic Review Discourse 2012–2017'. *International Journal of Human Rights*, 25(5): 45–58.

Chaney, P. 2021. 'An Institutionally Ableist State? Exploring Civil Society Perspectives on the Implementation of the Convention on the Rights of Persons with Disabilities in India'. *Journal of Civil Society*, 11 January.

Chaney, P. and S. Sahoo. 2020. 'Civil Society and the Contemporary Threat to Religious Freedom in Bangladesh'. *Journal of Civil Society*, 16(3): 191–215.

Cohen, J. and A. Arato. 1992. *Civil Society and Political Theory.* Cambridge: The MIT Press.

Comaroff, J.L. and J. Comaroff. 1999. 'Introduction'. In *Civil Society and the Political Imagination in Africa,* edited by J.L. Comaroff and J. Comaroff, 1–43, Chicago: The University of Chicago Press.

De Tocqueville, A. 1835 [1956]. *Democracy in America*, edited by R.D. Heffner, New York: Mentor.

Farzana, K.F. 2009. 'An Artificial Minority: The Stateless Biharis in Bangladesh'. *Journal of Muslim Minority Affairs*, 29(2): 223–235.

Gramsci, A. 1971 [1953]. *Selections from Prison Notebooks*, translated by Q. Hoare and G.N. Smith. New York: International Publishers.

Guru, G. 2005. 'Citizenship in Exile: A Dalit Case'. In *Civil Society, Public Sphere and Citizenship,* edited by R. Bhargava and H. Reifeld, 260–276. New Delhi: Sage Publications.

Habermas, J. 1987 [1981]. *Theory of Communicative Action, Volume Two: Lifeworld and System: A Critique of Functionalist Reason*, translated by Thomas A. McCarthy. Boston, MA: Beacon Press.

Holston, J. and A. Appadurai. 1996. 'Cities and Citizenship'. *Public Culture,* 8(2): 187–204.

Hudson, W., Q. Fahimul and T. Yutaka (eds). 2015. *Civil Society in Asia: In Search of Democracy and Development in Bangladesh*. Farnham: Ashgate.

Jayal, N.G. 2013. *Citizenship and its Discontents: An Indian History.* Cambridge: Harvard University Press.

Jenkins, L.D. 2019. *Religious Freedom and Mass Conversion in India.* Philadelphia: University of Pennsylvania Press.

Jensen, M. 2006. 'Concepts and Conceptions in Civil Society'. *Journal of Civil Society*, 2(1): 39–56.

Katyaini, S., M. Van Wessel and S. Sahoo. 2021. 'Representation by Development Organisations: Evidence from India and Implications for

Inclusive Development'. *Journal of Environment and Development*, 30(1): 98–123.

Klug, H. 2000. 'Contextual Citizenship'. *Indiana Journal of Global Legal Studies*, 7(2): 567–574.

Kumar, K. 1993. 'Civil Society: An Inquiry into the Usefulness of an Historical Term'. *British Journal of Sociology*, 44(3): 375–395.

Lewis, D. 2013. 'Civil Society and the Authoritarian State: Cooperation, Contestation and Discourse'. *Journal of Civil Society*, 9(3): 325–340.

Lister, R. 2003. *Citizenship: Feminist Perspectives*. New York: Palgrave Macmillan.

Marshall, T.H. 1950. *Citizenship and Social Class and Other Essays.* Cambridge: Cambridge University Press.

Naqvi, F. and Sadbhavna Trust. 2018. *Working with Muslims: Beyond Burqa and Triple Talaq Stories of Development and Everyday Citizenship in India.* New Delhi: Three Essays Collective.

Office of the High Commissioner for Human Rights (OHCHR). 2018. *United Nations Human Rights Management Plan 2018–21*. Geneva: United Nations.

Ong, A. 1999. *Flexible Citizenship: The Cultural Logics of Transnationality.* Durham: Duke University Press.

Polanyi, K. 2001 [1944]. *The Great Transformation: The Political and Economic Origins of Our Time.* Boston, MA: Beacon Press.

Prakash, A. 2001. *Jharkhand: Politics of Development and Identity.* Hyderabad: Orient Longman.

Rizvi, G. 1994. 'Democracy, Governance and Civil Society in South Asia'. *The Pakistan Development Review*, 33(4): 593–624.

Rudolph, S.H. 2000. 'Civil Society and the Realm of Freedom'. *Economic and Political Weekly*, 35(20): 1762–1769.

Sahoo, S. 2006. 'Civil Society, Citizenship and Subaltern Counterpublics in Post-Colonial India'. In *Sociological Perspectives on Globalization*, edited by A.K. Sahoo, 57–88. Delhi: Kalpaz Publications.

________. 2013. *Civil Society and Democratization in India: Institutions, Ideologies and Interests*. London: Routledge.

________. 2017. 'Market Liberalism, Marginalised Citizens and Countermovements in India'. *Asian Studies Review*, 41(1): 1–19.

Sahoo, S. 2018. *Pentecostalism and Politics of Conversion in India*. New Delhi: Cambridge University Press.

________. 2019. 'The Multiple Faces of Civil Society in India'. In *Civil Society in Global South*, edited by Palash Kamruzzaman, 104–119. London: Routledge.

Strachan, G., A. Adikaram and P. Kailasapathy. 2015. 'Gender (In)Equality in South Asia: Problems, Prospects and Pathways'. *South Asian Journal of Human Resources Management,* 2(1): 1–11.

Turner, B. 2017. 'Contemporary Citizenship: Four Types'. *Journal of Citizenship and Globalisation Studies*, 1(1): 10–23.

United Nations Convention on the Elimination of All Forms of Discrimination against Women. 2000. *Consideration of Reports Submitted by States Parties under Article 18 of the Convention - Initial Report of India*. Geneva: UN. CEDAW/C/SR.453.

USCIRF. 2020. *Annual Report.* Washington, D.C.: USCIRF Publications.

________. 2018. *Annual Report.* Washington, D.C.: USCIRF Publications.

Varshney, A. 2002. *Ethnic Conflict and Civic Life: Hindus and Muslims in India.* New Haven: Yale University Press.

1

Civil Society, Gender and Citizenship Rights: Complexities and Challenges Facing the Women's Movement in Today's India

B. Rajeshwari

Civil society, gender and citizenship rights have complex shades in the context of India. The three as separate concepts have acquired contested meanings complicating their relationship with each other. A lot of the literature on civil society in India has dealt with the subject as a response to the Western understanding of civil society and weaved the concept within the liberal democratic space (Chandhoke, 2007; Mahajan, 1999; Betteille, 2001). Yet, as some scholars argue (Rudolph, 2004; Sahoo, 2013), civil society in the Indian context is not always about organisations/movements advancing democratic, liberal values as has been understood in the west. There are many organisations in the civil sphere whose activities strengthen fundamentalist and extremist views; in consequence shrinking democratic spaces and voices. Gender rights are not just about men and women but about transgender identities and 'queer community'. Similarly, gender issues are no longer restricted to heterosexual men and women but also now extended to gays, lesbians, sex workers and others, resulting in the expansion of what we understand by gender.

The same trajectory is true of citizenship where several new rights are being extended to citizens (right to information, right to education, etc.). For instance, the Right to Information Act, 2005, gives Indian citizens access to information about any public authority or institution, including non-government organisations substantially funded by the government. Similarly, the Right to Education Act implemented in 2010 makes education for children between the age of 6 and 14 a fundamental right. At the same time, there is further contestation over who can claim to be a citizen, given the current developments surrounding the enactment of Citizenship Amendment Act and the National Registration Council in India. The Citizenship Amendment Act seeks to include new groups within the ambit of citizenship on the basis of their religious identity. But it leaves significant questions unanswered for the minority religious groups (George, 2019). All these factors serve to underline the dynamic, complex and challenging relationship between civil society, gender and citizenship in today's India.

Given the complex shades to civil society, gender and citizenship, it is impossible to explore all aspects of their evolving relationship at the start of the 21st century. The chapter, therefore, focuses in bringing forward some of the complexities facing civil society organisations (CSOs) in India while they work to advance gender and citizenship rights. Specific attention is given to the multiple and plural voices in the women's movement/organisations/groups that claim to advance gender and citizenship rights. *Inter alia*, the following discussion considers what challenges emerge when different groups within civil society seek legitimacy to advance gender and citizenship rights. It asks, how does a fragmented and significantly diverse civil society impact the claims of legitimacy for CSOs. Thus, in exploring the complex nature of civil society, the chapter addresses issues of legitimacy that most organisations and movements face irrespective of their ideological base and character. As the discussion proceeds, the chapter argues that increasing participation by one kind of movement or organisation can result in undermining the legitimacy of other organisations and their action repertoires (Porta, 2013). There are new forms, types and methods of actions that movements and organisations adapt and these tend to question the earlier forms. In this way, the chapter highlights that a central challenge to legitimacy is often faced by movements and organisations associated with the contested frameworks and claims of 'gender' (Tilly, 1977). This is particularly evident in the context of India where multiple identities and intersectionalities are at play and CSOs often struggle to address them all. The fact that women, men, transgender and the queer community are also entangled in other identity formulations like caste, tribe, religion, class and rural–urban. These tend to overlap with the gender identities, thereby, creating different formulations of what entails gender equality, the ways and methods to achieve the same.

The chapter is divided into three sections. The first critically reflects on the role of the women's movement in advancing the gender and citizenship rights along with questions about their legitimacy. The second and the third section discuss two key issues that question the legitimacy of women-led civil society movements and organisations. Specifically, the second section deals with the rise of right-wing groups led by and/or supported by women. In turn, we consider how these pose a challenge to women's groups/movements that are based on democratic values and liberal principles. The third section brings out a more complex shade to the issue of legitimacy. It explores how organisational/social movement legitimacy is possible when civil society activism is driven around the decisions of liberal democratic state institutions, such as the judiciary. In this context, the chapter discusses the case of the Muslim Personal Law and the Muslim women-led movement against Triple Talaq. In the face of questions being raised over their legitimacy, the section looks at the future prospects of women-led CSOs that work to advance gender and citizenship rights.

In making these arguments and claims, this chapter conceptually draws from feminist studies and writings that bring complex realities to the fore[1] while examining critically their own movements in advancing gender rights in India. The following discussion engages with the differences and diverse voices within feminism that range from white, liberal, socialist, north/south, coloured and Marxist feminisms. All of these give space for a dialogue and, therefore, a scope for new ways of approaching concepts like civil society (Deo, 2018). A critical feminist lens also allows us to reflect on some of the complexities and dichotomies involved within civil society groups and organisations that claim to advance rights of women and other groups who have been marginalised on grounds of their gender.

There are two other reasons for the current analytical approach. First, feminist writings and scholars have tried to grapple with the subject for some time now whilst other studies on civil society do not particularly engage with the relationship between gender and citizenship rights (Menon, 1998; Rajan, 2000; Sinha, 2003; Chari, 2009). Second, most CSOs that claim to advance gender rights have aligned with feminist ideas either directly or even indirectly. For instance, right-wing women's organisations in India despite their differences with feminists in ideology are certainly closer to them in their functional activities which includes running of charities, community service, child care, medical service for the poor, running schools and intervening in domestic abuse (Bedi, 2006). There are also structural and issue-based similarities between the right-wing organisations and other women's organisations (Deo, 2018). Thus, they have similarities in function/activities even if not in ideology. This makes it more important to draw from a diverse range of extant feminist writings and understand the ways in which they have explained the challenge of completely opposing ideologies to have similarities in form and also the participation of women in large numbers in civil society activism that do not believe in inclusive politics. Feminist studies have in various ways questioned the relevance of concepts like citizenship understood in liberal individualist terms in advancing women's rights (Pateman, 1989; Devenish, 2019). All these reasons make feminist studies the main conceptual framework to explain the challenges to legitimacy that CSOs confront while trying to advance equal citizenship and rights based on gender.

Women's Movement and Challenges to Legitimacy

The struggle for equal rights and citizenship claims based on gender has over the years been led in India primarily by the women's movement—comprising diverse organisations and groups (Krishnaraj, 2003; Subramanian, 2004). The Indian women's movement is most often referred to 'activities of hundreds of women's organisations with their own understandings of women's oppression and ways to counteract them' (Agnew, 1997). These organisations range from women's departments within the state bureaucracy to professional women's organisations, women's branches of political parties and trade unions to those dealing within specific issues like environment, anti-trafficking, etc. (Kumar, 1989). They have been joined by other women-led movements like the sex workers' group and LGBTQ movement. Overall, the women's movement has sustained the demand for gender equal inclusive rights and citizenship since independence. Yet, we know that the women's movement is not homogenous and there are many plural voices that are a part of it. The Indian women's movement has several streams of ideological thought and varying strategies (Gandhi and Shah, 1992). There are several divisions within the women's movement based on their ideology, caste, class, region and religion (Subramanian, 2004). These divisions have existed right from the 1960s when the women's movement started emerging in some shape and form in contemporary times (Khullar, 2005). Some of these divisions are based on urban-rural, feminist movements that draw from west as against other women's organisations/movements that distance themselves from Western influences. There have been several moments of ideological, methodical and processual differences among the different organisations that come within the ambit of women's movement but there has also been an overall consensus on the patriarchal and oppressive ways in which women undergo margnalisation, which needs to be addressed.

Among these components, religious divisions threaten the existence and legitimacy of civil society and its activities in an increasing politically constrained, yet notionally liberal democratic, civic space. The rise of fundamentalist voices appropriating the language of equal rights for women and large number of women becoming this voice has in serious ways questioned the activities of women's groups and movements that function according to democratic values. But this challenge seems to be far from answered by the feminists themselves. On the one hand, feminists have argued that one of the greatest challenges faced by the Indian Women's Movement since the 1990s is the co-option of their practices and discourses by 'forces that are inimical to feminist ends and progressive ideals' (Roy, 2015; Menon, 2004; Sangari, 2007; Tharu and Niranjana, 1994). The right-wing women's organisations also undertake activities as other feminist-based women's organisations by running charitable trusts, giving medical care to women, intervention in domestic abuse situations. Thus, they are similar in form even if not in ideology to the women's organisations who situate themselves within progressive feminist politics. The Mahila Agadi (women's wing of the Shiv Sena) is an example of how the co-option of strategies and activities have occurred. But feminists would argue that co-option seems to be a simplistic explanation to what is happening now with the Indian Women's Movement in terms of the ideological confrontation and women leading organisations that do not shy away from taking extremist/violent/communal positions within the women's movement.

These developments need to deal with complexities within the Indian women's movement, which include arguments linked to agency and empowerment to explain the current challenges (Saheli, 1991). The fundamentalist voices, whether it is the Mahila Agadi in Mumbai, the Sevika Samiti or the Durga Vahini (the women's wing of the Vishwa Hindu Parishad [VHP]), have appropriated the language of rights and equality to strengthen patriarchal structures and, more significantly, created a strong base for themselves among marginalised women who are emerging as the new 'female citizens' (Batliwala and Dhanraj, 2007). The female citizens as opposed to women as citizens are willingly, through their own agency, taking a secondary status vis-à-vis male citizen. They are coming out in public spaces creating their own positions without critically questioning the gender inequalities and patriarchal structures and rather reinforcing them in significant ways. Accordingly, this chapter explores the challenge of co-option by women's organisations like Durga Vahini, Sevika Samiti, Hindu Mahila Sammelan and Mahila Aghadi who speak simultaneously of exclusion on the basis of religious identity and of inclusion by making space for women in public sphere alongside men. They also speak of equality in participation for women and of turning them into warriors and baton bearers of Hindu cultural tradition and practices. Their positioning of women as nodal points attracts large-scale membership from middle and lower middle-class women, threatens the legitimacy of the women's movement in advancing rights and equal citizenship on the basis of gender.

Another challenge for the women's movement emerges from its internal heterogeneity and the multiple voices that exist within the movement. The women's movement in India has historically been accused for excluding marginal voices. For instance, the women's movement after independence was viewed as indulging in stereotypical activities and not raising crucial issues concerning women, such as rising gender disparities in employment, health, education and political participation (Sen, 2000; Subramanian, 2004). The Indian women's movement particularly witnessed in the 1980s and 1990s the mushrooming of professional and transnational non-governmental organisations who specifically worked on issues related to women and gender justice. But, despite several varieties of organisations becoming a part of the women's movement, it struggled to include all sections of women who were facing marginalisation at multiple levels.

Despite these challenges, the women's movement played an important role, particularly since the 1970s, in foregrounding gender disparities and the need to address them.

A close study of the women's movement suggests the presence of several dichotomies. On the one hand, it seemed to take up issues linked to both urban and rural women while, on the other hand, it also seemed to create a divide between them (Kumar, 2015). The linkages were in recognition of oppressive patriarchal practices, the absence of women in public spaces, the cognisance of the violence against women and ways to counter them. The divide was apparent in the language of rights that the urban feminists spoke by locating women in the spectrum of individual rights which alienated the rural women and other women's rights' organisations for whom advancement of women's rights cannot be located outside their community rights. Similarly, it seemed to open the debate on public and private by taking on the state for its gender discriminatory personal laws. The women's movement and organisations have long argued in India as also in the West that gender justice and equal rights can only be realised when division of labour, oppressive practices in the private sphere are addressed alongside the lack of women's participation and gender equality in public sphere (including the state). Yet, the women's movement has struggled to give space to multiple realities of identities and cultural practices that exist while calling for reforming the personal laws. This has particularly been true when it is related to reforming the personal laws of the minority communities in India. The women's organisations like Forum against Oppression of Women and Working Group of Women's Rights, that aim to reform personal laws through state intervention, are a crossroads where they are being challenged for excluding the agency of the women whose rights they seek to advance.

In the case of women's movement, the notion of 'civil society' suggests that activism around equal citizenship based on gender is deeply entangled with other identities becoming more important for women themselves. The Temple Entry movement[2] in Sabarimala, backed by the Supreme Court's judgement, is a prominent example of the multiple ways in which a movement can be viewed by the members of the same community whose rights it claims to advance. In such situations, the legitimacy of the movement comes under serious question alongside the fact that some of these movements further reinforce patriarchal practices without being aware of doing it. Some of these issues are highlighted later in the chapter through the Sabarimala Temple entry movement.

The Growing Participation of Women in Communalist Activism

A serious challenge and complex reality that CSOs are currently facing is the participation and incorporation of women to advance agenda that are antithetical to democratic principles. What remains inexplicable is that a lot of this active participation happens through organisations working in civil society. This aspect is often less studied from the lens of a civil society subject because these organisations are viewed outside the purview of civil society, given their illiberal and sometimes even undemocratic foundations. The emergence of the right-wing political parties in India with ideological roots in nationalism, majoritarianism and religious conservatism has taken an active form since the 1990s—post the demolition of the Babri Masjid. In India, the politics of the right wing has been studied under the umbrella of what is termed Hindu nationalism and political parties like Bharatiya Janata Party (BJP), Shiv Sena and organisations like Rashtriya Swayamsevak Sangh (RSS), the VHP have ideological underpinnings in Hindu Nationalism (Ahmed and Balasubramanian, 2010). The mobilisational and advocacy strategies of some of these and their women's wing has become a serious challenge because of the growing membership and support base for rights-based civil society advocacy . Their uncontestable divine position attributed to women have generally posed a threat to the secular liberal politics that feminist organisations have historically aligned themselves with (Bedi, 2006).

A number of right-wing political parties—the Shiv Sena, BJP—in India have a women's wing (such as Shiv Sena's Mahila Aghadi, Durga Vahini) and they mobilise women on fundamentally religious lines. The Mahila Aghadi (translated as women first or women in front) was founded in 1985 and its strategies adopted in Mumbai can be useful to understand the problematic nature of gender identity that these organisations subscribe to. The Aghadi women and their organisation has an identical and parallel structure as that of the Shiv Sena, suggesting the equal positioning of the female vis-à-vis the male (Bedi, 2006). But, decision-making was in the hands of the male organisation—Shiv Sena—which was viewed as hierarchically above the Mahila Aghadi. The Mahila Agadi, like other right-wing women's organisations, has given space for women to engage actively in social causes and give them scope for political activism (Batliwala and Dhanraj, 2007). This political activism of the Aghadi women can be seen through their assertion of the Shiv Sena card by explicitly taking a violent form through local patronage systems and ensuring that 'things get done' (Bedi, 2006).

The members of Aghadi are primarily from middle and lower middle class—slum dwellers of Mumbai with a strong sense of religious and cultural identity of being a Hindu and a Maharashtrian. They also belong to the migrant families who moved from the rural areas of Maharashtra in search for better opportunities to the urban Mumbai (Sen, 2006). Thus, they participate in public sphere through engagement in resolving several types of issues like domestic abuse, police harassment, medical facility for women, etc. Their presence in the public sphere is deeply connected to the reshaping of the private realm of their women members. In multiple ways they challenge the existing unequal gender practices and yet subscribe to their role as subordinates to the Shiv Sena, which is dominated by the men. These women were assumed to be passive recipients and implementers of the masculine agenda of the Sena. But, several studies on the Mahila Aghadi and their members suggest that they are far from passive. These women have in their own way transformed how the private practices and patriarchal roles are challenged in public spaces and are reconstructed (Sharma, 2019; Sen, 2006) This begs the question—how can issues of gender and patriarchy be viewed for women's rights when organisations like the Aghadi bring modernist values within a framework of patriarchal values (Sarkar, 1991)? The Aghadi gives its women members political, public and even leadership roles—something that other feminist movements have been talking about all along. The participation and roles in public spaces does not mean these women critique class, caste and patriarchy in all forms and remain silent on diverse aspects of these issues and more significantly it encourages women to represent themselves on communal lines (Sarkar, 1991). In her study on the Aghadi women, Sen (2006) points to the 'New Freedom (*Nayi Azadi*) that they experience without toppling the patriarchal balances within their society'.

The conundrum for feminists and civil society scholars is—can women's participation be viewed as instrumentalisation of these women for a fundamentalist/communalist cause or can it be explained as women exercising their active agency as citizens and participating in public spaces to bring about social and political transformations? Women members of Mahila Aghadi exercise their agency and choice in consciously choosing the membership of an organisation that encourages them to use violent demeanour, language and even action when required. A more central issue is understanding the way women's participation in large numbers in the activities of Mahila Aghadi and similar organisations rearticulates gender attributes that, according to several scholars, maintains the power status quo within the society and reaffirms patriarchal practices, giving them legitimacy (Kapur and Cossman, 1993). When these women undertake masculine forms of action through the use of violence and threats, they legitimise these methods vis-à-vis those that are located in liberal and democratic forms. Even before the Aghadi was formally founded, the Sena women had developed an aggressive public image as picketers, abuse brigades and violent demonstrators (Sen, 2006). They are viewed by other CSOs and scholars as speaking about women's rights at a more superficial level, in ways that further and strengthen patriarchal norms and structures (Hasan, 2009). But, to dismiss them and their methods would not provide an understanding of the legitimacy they receive with increasing membership and support.

There is now a critical reflection by feminists on whether women's participation in fundamentalist and communalist activism can be viewed as 'false consciousness' and the instrumentalisation of these women to a larger ideological goal of the Hindu right. The Sena for instance was strategic in the formulation of its women's wing and several male members felt that the party 'needed a progressive image' (Sen, 2006) and women's participation would help the party garner their support and build their image that promoted equality for women. It is naïve not to recognise the agency that women exercise while participating in activities and movements that clearly support goals that cannot be aligned with democratic values (Bedi, 2006; Batliwala and Dhanraj, 2007; Sen, 2007). It is important to recognise this agency alongside a response to these groups that come from other democratic women's groups. This agency can be contextual (Mahmood, 2006), but, nevertheless, it is based on a conscious decision that women make when they decide to be a part of these movements. When the Aghadi women members resolve their everyday issues like sexual harassment while travelling in local train and the organisation gives them the authority to do so, they view themselves as people who can decide and change their oppressive situations (Bedi, 2006).

This complex reality suggests that gender becomes a focal point not just for those civil society groups that seek to advance gender rights through democratic principles and norms, engaging in peaceful activism. On the contrary, gender also becomes a focal point for other civil society groups and movements who engage in undemocratic principles, engaging, when required, in violent activism. The Mahila Aghadi constantly use the Sena threat while dealing with domestic abuse, sexual harassment in local trains and sometimes even the use of violence against religious and ethnic 'others' (Bedi, 2006). But when they make gender their focal point, it tends to undermine the legitimacy of organisations and movements based on democratic principles and norms. When gender becomes central to these groups and movements, then it poses the challenge of resurgent patriarchal practices and leads to the redefinition of the boundaries of citizenship. They speak for gender equality at a superficial level and yet are also able to speak to the sensibilities of women who join them in large numbers, consciously choosing violent methods over the peacefully deliberated path advocated by the progressive women's movement.

Resurgent Patriarchal Practices and Redefining the Boundaries of Citizenship

There are CSOs constantly working to challenge patriarchy and patriarchal practices. One of the ways in which feminist organisations do this is through capacity development training at both individual and organisational levels. An important element of these has been training women and men about gender equality. Such training began in India in the mid-1980s with strong links to the women's movement (Gilbertson and Sen, 2017). It started with consciousness raising programmes such as the World Development Programme of Rajasthan and Mahila Samakhya (Gilbertson and Sen, 2017). Women's movement since its inception in India has challenged in various ways patriarchy through demands for property right for women, demanding revisions in existing legal provisions available for rape victims, leading movements against dowry and widow burning and demanding reforms in domestic laws to address issues like domestic violence. These have brought positive transformations in advancing gender rights. Such endeavours have brought women closer to equal citizenship.

Women in India, as in many countries in South Asia, continue to be under-represented in both electoral and non-electoral forms of representation. The participation of women and their engagement through electoral and other means is an important marker for the 'maturity and efficacy of democracy in a country' (Rai, 2011). The Indian Women's movement has tried over the years to position women and their concerns in discussions, debates and policy reflections to ensure that gender equality can be advanced and civil society can play an influential role in achieving this. Yet, not all moments/junctures led by women's organisations that speak of bringing women to public spaces and increase their participation challenge unequal patriarchal practices. The earlier discussion on women's growing participation in violent activism points to this aspect in several ways.

Such movements constantly question boundaries of citizenship where women become agents that actively support reducing citizenship rights for other groups. An example of this is the active involvement of women in Maharashtra questioning the presence of skilled labour from other states in Mumbai, thus, reducing the employment opportunities of men from their own state. In giving this support, women made a conscious choice to become agents of a movement that was reinforcing patriarchal understanding of who can be a skilled labourer and also undermining the citizenship rights of groups who were equally entitled to it. The simultaneous presence of two types of organisations in the women's movement—one that challenges patriarchy and another that seeks to reinforce it—creates a contest between the two bringing new types of questions for gender and citizenship along with the boundaries that define them. The presence of these two different kinds of parallel movements/

organisations also questions their overall legitimacy in trying to pursue rights and equal citizenship on the basis of gender.

The Challenge of Intersectionality and Diversity to Advancing Gender Rights

A significant part of civil society activism and advocacy in India has been centred on challenging the personal laws of different faiths that undermine the rights of women as individuals. But, such attempts by CSOs amount to a formidable challenge as often the question of who gets included and excluded in these movements and how they position themselves becomes a vital area of contestation. Such a contestation again raises legitimacy questions for organisations that are working to challenge the personal laws.

The attempt to bring legal intervention in Muslim Personal Law by organisations is a case in point. The state's response to the Shah Bano case[3] and its bowing down to the communitarian forces that clearly undermined the rights of women as individuals forced the women's movement to rethink its strategy for greater gender rights (Schneider, 2009). Some of the Muslim women's organisations like Awaaz-e-Niswan, All India Muslim Women's Rights Network, Bharatiya Muslim Mahila Andolan (BMMA) were constituted over the years and sought to work for Muslim women though they never claimed to exclusively work only for women of one particular community (Schneider, 2009). For example, the Awaaz-e-Niswan (voice of women) 'calls itself a vibrant feminist collective of students, academicians, activists from women's movement and women who daily confront violations of their rights and evolve strategies to combat them'.[4]

The Niswan was formed in 1985 by Shehnaaz who was given a unilaterally divorce on the basis of Muslim Personal Law. She got together with other Muslim women who also had similar experiences and she, along with the others, filed a petition against the Muslim

Personal Law. The Niswan works on cases related to dowry, giving relief to women victims of communal violence and one of their key objectives is to bring educational, economic and social awareness among Muslim women so that they can have their own voice against the several forms of violence they undergo. These organisations were mostly formed around or after the Shah Bano case with the intention to have grassroot-level activities for marginalised women and reinterpret their own laws and seek solutions for these within their own personal law. There was unease when the demand for Uniform Civil Code was appropriated by the Hindu Nationalists as a way to come to power and, therefore, several women's organisations tried distancing themselves from such a demand (Hasan, 2000).

The BJP in 1998 promised to implement the Uniform Civil Code if it came to power. It had till then used the issue to challenge the Congress Party's secular politics by stating that their politics was about appeasing the Muslim community. The party could not implement this in 1998 after coming to power, as it did not have the sufficient majority to raise the issue (Hasan, 2000). The BJP's taking this up in 2014 after coming to power became paradoxical for women's organisations and forced the Muslim women's organisations to rework and rethink their strategies with respect to their stand in relation to the issue of the Muslim Personal Law, the subsequent abolition of Triple Talaq and whether a Uniform Civil Code can be an answer for more gender parity. Even organisations like All India Democratic Women's Association (AIDWA), which earlier promoted a Uniform Civil Code, now favour a gradual change in personal laws. These women's organisations have now carved a separate path for themselves in many ways distancing themselves from secular liberal women's movement as they feel that the solutions for their problems need to be sought within their own personal laws and a reinterpretation of it. They faced, on the one hand, the challenges of their strategies and demands being co-opted by the right-wing to correlate them with the Uniform Civil Code. On the other hand, their demands were also used in a media-driven campaign against their own religion, making them critically reflect on what they wanted and how they planned to work towards their demands (Deo, 2018).

The Muslim women's organisations like BMMA have suggested that there is no opposition between the Muslim Personal Law and the Constitution of India and the problem lies in the interpretation of the Quran. This stand seems to be well thought out with an intention to represent the rights of Muslim women and move them closer to a gender-just society. It also suggests a move towards equal citizenship rights for these women (Sur, 2018). Nevertheless, this stand is not without its own set of challenges and setbacks. From where do these women's organisations draw their legitimacy to represent the Muslim women? A critical reflection of their work by scholars has raised questions over their stand on behalf of all the women of the community, considering that several women still rely on the multiple legal actors when faced with conflicts related to personal matters (Chakrabarti and Ghosh, 2017). These women take the help of Sharia courts, clergy, women's organisations and religious organisations and the mediating role of local courts is something that has been recognised even by the Supreme Court (Sur, 2018; Chakrabarti and Ghosh, 2017).

A large number of cases related to unilateral divorce are registered in Mahila Adalats (women's courts) which are convened by organisations like All India Muslim Women's Personal Law Board (AIMWPLB) (Vatuk, 2008). A very small percentage of Muslim women bring legal cases to the regular courts with the aim of settling personal matters. Yet, BMMA is one of the petitioners questioning Triple Talaq in a regular court, claiming to represent a majority of Muslim women in India. In many ways, the case of Triple Talaq on the one hand is a celebration of the agency of Muslim women who during the Shah Bano case depended on other organisations to represent their case but, by the Shyara Bano case (2016), they were represented by women's organisations formed by their own community women. It still raises complex issues linked to gender justice for Muslim women as the recent law criminalising Triple Talaq passed in both the houses of Parliament is feared to push these women far away from the regular courts since it threatens to subject their men to criminal acts; the repercussions of which Muslim women are not prepared to deal with.

This case highlights two essential issues: (a) The emergence of Muslim women's organisations largely representing issues of Muslim women after the Shah Bano case as many in the community felt that a pan-Indian women's movement was not equipped to deal with their problems that lay within their own personal laws. It shows the failed attempt of women's movement in India to incorporate the issues of Muslim women within their larger narrative and movement. (b) The formation of separate women's organisations by Muslim women has not meant that their women are closer to gender justice, given the state's interpretation of their demands and struggles. The question of gender equality and citizenship rights of Muslim women are woven within their community laws and any attempt to divorce the two remains problematic. Through the case of Muslim women's network, the chapter shows that these organisations are on the one hand demonstrating new forms of political agency for Muslim women where their religious identity does not become compromised; while on the other hand, the chapter also argues that such an attempt of redefining the agency of Muslim women has not meant that questions are not being raised over their right to represent all the women in the community.

Multiple identities of a marginalised group, resulting in challenging movements and causes for gender equality, is witnessed in the case of other religious groups in India. The Sabarimala Temple has had a practice of restricting the entry of females aged between 10 and 50 into the premises of the temple. The practice has been followed now for several years on the belief that Lord Ayyappa was a celibate and only those who had 'observed penance', that is, the purity period of 41 days could enter the temple. The women in the restricted age group could not observe this penance and, thus, their entry has been restricted for several years now (Singh, 2016). The practice was challenged in the Kerala High Court and in 1991 the court upheld the restriction. The court was of the view that it only restricted a particular group of women and not all women from entry and, thus, the principle of right to equality cannot be applied in this case.

The Supreme Court recently gave a verdict on the case in favour of women's rights groups and said that women within the restricted age group should be allowed entry to the temple as it restricted their fundamental right to equality. The Sabarimala Temple movement was led by an organisation called the Bhumata Brigade[5] and it has also witnessed momentum because of the support from several women activists from within and outside Kerala. It is interesting to note that while the Bhumata Brigade has led the campaign for temple entry in Sabarimala, this is not a movement where only one organisation or a single group has contributed. The 'Happy to Bleed' campaign led by a number of women and supported by a significant amount of men was also a way of questioning the authority of the Sabarimala Temple in denying entry to women who were of menstruating age (Khurana, 2017).

The demand to enter the temple in Sabarimala is clearly for the 'believers' and the temple authority views it as a challenge to social norms and religious practices. Following the Supreme Court order, there has been resistance from the community where a campaign has been led against the entry of women in Sabarimala. In this case, while the state government has extended support for the women willing to enter the temple, the central government has questioned the entry, suggesting that the courts should not interfere in the religious matters. This has not stopped women activists led by different groups from forming a human chain to support the temple entry of women in Sabarimala. This reflects part of the reality related to this movement. The other part is also about stiff resistance from civil society groups which include women who clearly do not identify with this movement and view it as a threat to their beliefs/practices, identifying themselves closer to the community ties.

While, several women's groups regarded Sabarimala as a movement speaking of equal rights for women, it left uncomfortable questions by the end of the episode. One of the central questions raised during the temple entry for women in Sabarimala led by women's rights organisations was: who are they representing? Are they representing a large section of women of their community or a miniscule percentage who want to enter this temple? Also, is this movement not reasserting patriarchy in significant ways by fighting to enter a temple that is largely a symbol of patriarchal practices, considering that men perform all the rituals and define the laws of the temple? In making a demand for the right to enter the temple, these organisations were also viewed as speaking for a particular caste of women (upper caste Hindu women) who wanted to enter the temple and in doing so they excluded the struggles of the non-savarna women. This exclusion and the sense of alienation that emerges for the most marginalised women make gender equality more complicated and challenging than it seems. A celebration of rights for few can create a sense of deprivation for the other as there is so much diversity among the issues that women face across the country, considering their intersectional ties that it becomes challenging for CSOs to advance rights across gender.

What Is Gained and Lost for the Women's Movement?

The complex nature of gender and citizenship rights makes it essential to examine what impact these challenges to legitimacy have for the women's movement. The realisation that their activities, methods and strategies can be adopted by different sets of civil society groups whose values are completely opposed to the sensibilities of the progressive women's movement can be counted as an important gain. The realisation of co-option makes women's movement conscious of the reality that even fundamentalist groups operate within the civil society space and, therefore, they need to carefully choose their strategies and causes. It also pushes the women's movement to devise new methods and strategies to gain legitimacy among those who consciously choose to join right wing groups over the women's groups that seek to advance gender rights through liberal and democratic practices.

The cases discussed in this chapter are reflective of the fact that the women's movement is deeply fragmented and has become more so since the 1990s. In some ways, the fragmented nature of women's movement needs to be celebrated to understand that there is space for varied civil society activism and there are multiple ways in which the advancing of gender rights can be imagined. But there are also costs, not least the shrinking space for the progressive character of women's movement that operates within liberal values and democratic principles. The deeply fragmented women's movement quells the possibility of a pan-Indian understanding of the role of civil society in advancing gender and citizenship rights. This has meant the existence of several smaller local movements instead of a singular movement that can speak to all issues linked to gender rights within the country. This plural nature of the women's movement can be viewed as a gain, allowing differences to exist. Yet, it makes the women's movement weak, by raising suspicions regarding its ability to represent all sections of marginalised women in India.

In short, we are witnessing an ongoing battle that has become stronger in the recent years with the coming of fundamentalist voices in civil society. In a country that is undergoing a formidable challenge with regard to the citizenship rights and protests with regard to the passing of controversial laws related to citizenship, the role of women's movement becomes significant. Women's groups and organisations as was witnessed in Shaheen Bagh came out on the streets to demonstrate against the Citizenship Amendment Act. There were also parallel visuals of women participating in demonstrations that were held to support the Act. These contesting realities/repertoires determine the complexities linked to civil society activism in India and particularly with regard to questions of gender equality.

Concluding Remarks

This chapter highlights some of the central challenges that emerge when the CSOs try to advance rights and equal citizenship based on gender. In doing so, it speaks about the contemporary challenges that have emerged in advancing the rights of women. Similar issues can be traced while studying the course of civil society initiatives to advance the rights of transgender people and an expansion of rights related to sexuality. The chapter makes the argument that initiatives from CSOs towards equal rights on the basis of gender cannot be accepted uncritically. It requires critical reflections on women's and feminist movements to highlight the emerging challenges and address key questions.

Feminist scholars and studies have been self-critical of their own movements and, therefore, much of the criticism flows from this body of work. Nevertheless, there are unanswered questions related to women's agency in participating in fundamentalist extremist movements, in advancing exclusionary practices within the women's movement undermining intersectional ties and, above all, leading to a resurgent patriarchy that on several occasions gets tacit support from women's organisations themselves. This chapter primarily addresses the debate on civil society, gender and citizenship by focusing on the internal debates and challenges emerging from within civil society for women's movement. These internal debates and challenges certainly raise questions around the legitimacy of women's movement and its relevance for advancing the rights and citizenship on the basis of gender.

Notes

1. Even in India, there are several differences among feminists which gets reinforced in the writings of Dalit feminists as against 'educated-urban' feminists time and again. See Rege (1998).
2. The Sabarimala Case came before the Supreme Court in the year 2006 by way of a Public Interest Litigation under Article 32 of the Constitution of India. The Association of Young Lawyers were the petitioners of the case and filed it for the entry of female devotees between the age group of 10 and 50 at the Lord Ayyappa Temple at Sabrimala (Kerala) which has been denied to them on the basis of certain custom and usage.
3. *Shah Bano vs Mohammed Ahmed Khan* came to the Supreme Court for hearing in 1981 where Shah Bano was divorced by her husband in 1978 and he was refusing to pay her the monthly maintenance of ₹200. The Court ruled in favour of Shah Bano in 1985, granting allowance to Shah Bano under the Criminal Procedure Code. Shayara Bano along with four other Muslim women filed a petition in Supreme Court in 2016 against the Islamic practice of talaq-e-bidat (triple talaq), challenging it to be unconstitutional in not recognising the fundamental right to equality as enshrined in Article 14 of the Indian Constitution and Article 15(1) (prohibition of discrimination including on the ground of gender). The Supreme Court gave the verdict on 22 August 2017 where it held triple talaq to be unconstitutional.
4. See http://www.niswaan.org/.
5. Bhumata Brigade is a Pune-based non-governmental organisation, founded by Trupti Desai, dedicated to fighting against women and corruption. It was founded in 2010 and is best known for its protests against the banning of women from places of worship. It has led campaigns against Shani Shingnapur Temple in Ahmednagar, Maharashtra and Haji Ali Dargah in Mumbai, Maharashtra. They also led the movement for entering the Sabarimala Devasthana Temple in Kerala.

References

Agnew, Vijay. 1997. 'The West in Indian Feminist Discourse and Practice'. *Women's Studies International Forum*, 20(1): 3–19.

Ahmed, Zahid and Rajeshwari Balasubramanian. 2010. *Extremism in Pakistan and India: The Case of Jamaat-i-Islami and Shiv Sena*, RCSS Policy Studies 50. Colombo: Regional Center for Strategic Studies.

Batliwala, Srilatha and D. Dhanraj. 2007. 'Gender Myths That Instrumentalize Women: A View from the Indian Front Line'. *Feminisms in Development: Contradictions, Contestations and Challenges*, 35(4): 11–18.

Bedi, T. 2006. 'Feminist Theory and the Right-wing: Shiv Sena Women Mobilize Mumbai'. *Journal of International Women's Studies*, 7(4): 51–68.

Beteille, Andrei. 2001. 'Civil Society and the Good Society'. *Sociological Bulletin*, 50(2): 286–307.

Chakrabarti, A. and S. Ghosh. 2017. 'Judicial Reform vs Adjudication of Personal Law'. *Economic and Political Weekly*, 52(49): 13.

Chandhoke, Neera. 2007. 'Civil Society'. *Development in Practice*, 17(4–5): 607–614.

Chari, A. 2009. 'Gendered Citizenship and Women's Movement'. *Economic and Political Weekly*, 64(17): 47–57.

Deo, Nandini (ed.) 2018. *Postsecular Feminisms: Religion and Gender in Transnational Context*. London: Bloomsbury Academic.

Devenish, A. 2019. *Debating Women's Citizenship in India 1930–1960*. New Delhi: Bloomsbury Publishing.

Gandhi, N. and N. Shah. 1992. *The Issues at Stake—Theory and Practice in the Contemporary Women's Movement in India*. New Delhi: Kali for Women.

George, V. 2019. 'Citizenship Amendment Act—The Fear Factor'. *The Hindu,* 17 December.

Gilbertson, A. and Rukmini Sen. 2017. 'Gender Training in Delhi'. Research Report submitted to University of Melbourne, Australia.

Hasan, Z. 2000. *Uniform Civil Code and Gender Justice in India. Contemporary India*: Transitions. New Delhi: Sage Publications.

Hasan, Zoya. 2010. 'Gender, Religion and Democratic Politics in India'. *Third World Quarterly*, 31(6): 939–954.

________. 2009. 'Gender, Religion and Democratic Politics in India'. A Report submitted for the project Religion, Politics and Gender

Equality to United Nations Research Institute for Social Development, Geneva.

Kapur, R. and B. Cossman. 1993. 'Communalising Gender/Engendering Community: Women, Legal Discourse and Saffron Agenda'. *Economic and Political Weekly*, 28(17): WS35–WS44.

Khullar, M. (ed.). 2005. *Writing the Women's Movement: A Reader*. New Delhi: Zubaan.

Khurana, N.A. 2017. 'Right to Pray and Gender Debate in India'. *Advances in Social Sciences Research Journal*, 4(17): 215–224.

Krishnaraj, M. 2003. 'Challenges before Women's Movement in a Changing Context'. *Economic and Political Weekly*, 38(43): 4536–4545.

_______. 2012. 'The Women's Movement in India: A Hundred Year History'. *Social Change*, 42(3): 325–333.

Kumar, Radha. 1989. 'Contemporary Indian Feminism'. *Feminist Review*, 33: 20–29.

_______. 2015. 'The Women's Movement in India'. *Indian Journal of Public Administration*, 61(3): 423–444.

Mahajan, Gurpreet. 1999. 'Civil Society and Its Avatars: What Happened to Freedom and Democracy?'. *Economic and Political Weekly*, 34 (20): 1188–1196.

Mahmood, Saba. 2006. 'Feminist Theory, Agency, and the Liberatory Subject: Some Reflections on the Islamic Revival in Egypt'. *Temenos*, 42(1): 31–71.

Menon, Nivedita. 1998. 'State/Gender/Community: Citizenship in Contemporary India.' *Economic and Political Weekly*, 33(5): PE3–PE10.

_______. 2004. *Recovering Subversion: Feminist Politics beyond the Law*. Chicago: University of Illinois Press.

Pateman, Carol. 1989. *The Disorder of Women: Democracy, Feminism and Political Theory*. Cambridge: Polity Press.

Porta, Della Donatella. 2013. 'Repertoires of Contention'. In *The Wiley-Blackwell Encyclopedia of Social and Political Movements*, edited by David A. Snow, 1–3, New York: Blackwell Publishing Ltd.

Rai, P. 2011. 'Electoral Participation of Women in India: Key Determinants and Barriers'. *Economic and Political Weekly*, 46(3): 47–55.

_______. 2017. 'Women's Participation in Electoral Politics in India: Silent Feminisation'. *South Asia Research*, 37(1): 58–77.

Rajan, R.S. 2000. 'Women between Community and State: Some Implications of the Uniform Civil Code Debates in India'. *Social Text*, 18(4): 55–82.

Rege, S. 1998. 'Dalit Women Talk Differently: A Critique of "Difference" Towards a Dalit Feminist Standpoint Position'. *Economic and Political Weekly*, 33(44): WS39–WS46.

Roy, S. 2015. 'The Indian Women's Movement: Within and beyond NGOization'. *Journal of South Asian Development*, 10(1): 96–117.

Rudolph, Suzanne. 2004. 'Is Civil Society the Answer?'. In *Interrogating Social Capital: The Indian Experience*, edited by Dwaipayan Bhattacharya, Niraja Gopal Jayal, Bishnu N. Mohapatra and Sudha Pai, 117–134, New Delhi: Sage Publications.

Saheli. 1991. *Development for Whom? A Critique of Women's Development Programs.* A Report on the development programmes in Rajasthan with a specific focus on the Ajmer district.

Sahoo, Sarbeswar. 2013. *Civil Society and Democratization in India: Institutions, Ideologies and Interests*. London and New York: Routledge.

Sangari, K. 2007. 'Shaping Pressures and Symbolic Horizons: The Women's Movement in India'. In *At the Cutting Edge: Essays in Honour of Kumari Jayawardena*, edited by N. De Mel and S. Thiruchandran, 36–67, New Delhi: Women Unlimited.

Sarkar, T. 1991. 'The Woman as Communal Subject: Rashtrasevika Samiti and Ram Janmabhoomi Movement'. *Economic and Political Weekly*, 26(35): 2057–2062.

Schneider, N.C. 2009. 'Islamic Feminism and Muslim Women's Rights Activism in India: From Transnational Discourse to Local Movement-or vice versa?'. *Journal of International Women's Studies*, 11(1): 56–71.

Sen, A. 2006. 'Reflecting on Resistance: Hindu Women "Soldiers" and the Birth of Female Militancy'. *Indian Journal of Gender Studies*, 13(1): 1–35.

________. 2007. *Shiv Sena Women: Violence and Communalism in a Bombay Slum*. Bloomington: Indiana University Press.

Sen, S. 2000. *Toward a Feminist Politics?: The Indian Women's Movement in Historical Perspective*. World Bank, Development Research Group/ Poverty Reduction and Economic Management Network.

Sharma, Kamini. 2019. 'The Mahila Aghadi: The Shiv Sena Women and Urban Politics'. *International Journal of Multidisciplinary Research Studies*, 1(3): 15–27.

Singh, Trishala. 2016. 'Women's Right to Access: Seeking Gender Equality in Places of Worship'. *Arts and Education International Research Journal*, 3(1): 107–110.

Sinha, K. 2003. 'Citizenship Degraded: Indian Women in a Modern State and a Pre-modern Society'. *Gender & Development*, 11(3): 19–26.

Subramanian, M. 2004. 'The Indian Women's Movement'. *Contemporary Sociology*, 33(6): 635–639.

Sur, E. 2018. 'Triple Talaq Bill in India: Muslim Women as Political Subjects or Victims?'. *Space and Culture, India*, 5(3): 5–12.

Tharu, S. and T. Niranjana. 1994. 'Problems for a Contemporary Theory of Gender'. *Social Scientist*, 22(3/4): 93–117.

Tilly, Charles. 1977. *Repertoires of Contention in America and Britain*, 1750–1830. Michigan: University of Michigan.

Vatuk, S. 2008. 'Islamic Feminism in India: Indian Muslim Women Activists and the Reform of Muslim Personal Law'. *Modern Asian Studies*, 42(2/3): 489–518.

2

Women's Rights and Social Movements in Bangladesh: The Changing Political Field*

Seuty Sabur

Women have always been active agents of change in Bengal. There were, and are, extraordinary revolutionaries who paved the way for millions of women, seizing the torch and leading the way in times of crisis; unfortunately, their transformative roles/power have not been adequately documented. The countless revolutionary women and men who made these social transformations possible were differentially located at the intersections of diverse classes, religions and ethnicities, motivated by diverse political agendas. They forced open the space for a feminist political field by setting examples with their lived politics, creating associations and resisting various oppressive regimes. The following discussion is a tribute to those countless ordinary women who lived extraordinary lives, translated the 'personal into political', nurtured a space for extraordinary dreams and found 'unity in diversity' within collective action. This chapter explores the diverse women's movements in Bangladesh over the past six decades, concentrating on women's agency and their shifting allegiance to the state.

* Part of this research was formulated under the mentorship of Raka Ray, during the faculty training workshop on writing and publishing at the Subir & Malini Chowdhury Center for Bangladesh Studies at UC Berkeley [Co-sponsored by American Institute for Bangladesh Studies (AIBS) and the Council of American Overseas Research Centers (CAORC)] in 2018. Further research was done under Global Challenges Research Funded Project #513744, titled 'Civil Society and Good Governance in India and Bangladesh', awarded by the Academy of Medical Sciences, UK, March 2018–August 2019. I am thankful to Elora Shehabuddin, Elora Halim Chowdhury, Dina Siddiqui, Firdous Azim, Nandini Deo, Paul Chaney and Sarbeswar Sahoo for their feedback on earlier drafts and Shehzad M. Arifeen for editorial assistance.

By putting the collective agency of these women at the centre, this chapter explores the politics they articulated for themselves, the trepidations they faced, as well as the elements that created the enabling environment in which they thrived. Despite the heterogeneity of experiences, the thread that bound them together was their fight for their rights, not least, the basic human right to exist as full citizens of the nation state. Excavating the archives of the pre- and the post-independence period in Bangladesh, drawing from repositories such as women's organisations' literature, oral histories, interviews and discussion from the workshop, this chapter situates the activists within the larger national-transnational political field. This chapter maps out the 'political field' in which the women's movement was (and is) embedded, by focusing on the coalitions initiated by the women's organisations and their negotiations with other actors, including other civil society groups, donors and UN agencies, non-governmental organisations (NGOs), political parties and the state. This account also casts light on how women's bodies have been used as sites of resistance. I explore the historical trajectories of these organisations in order to understand their radical pasts, how they defined human rights through their actions, the programmes they initiated and the challenges they faced. Attention also centres around the sequence of events that led to their 'deradicalisation' and, finally, I consider the possibility of articulating a feminist politics for human rights beyond the limits of the UN and the state. The following section explains the constituting factors shaping the political field, beginning with the anticolonial movements to contemporary women's movements in Bangladesh.

Women's Movement and the Political Field in Bangladesh

Pierre Bourdieu conceptualised the 'field' as a space where individual agency and forms of capital are at play, and manoeuvre in order to occupy a position within a socially constructed hierarchical structure (Bourdieu, 2002). My own analysis builds on Raka Ray's redefinition of the concept for use in the study of collectives. For Ray, '[a] field can be thought of as a structured, unequal, and socially constructed environment *within* which organisations are embedded and *to* which organisations and activists constantly respond' (Ray, 1999). Individual and collective actors within a field do not exist in a vacuum; rather, their actions are always 'relational' (Ray, 1999), and bear the burden of their predecessors' social relations. Despite this, however, they are also always equipped with a transformative agency that they use to change the field itself. Like Ray, I put collective agency at the centre of the ecosystem that these activists and revolutionaries occupy, mapping out the complex negotiations that women's organisations underwent in Bangladesh for over six decades, and the outcomes of such negotiations. I explore the kind of political field that made such organisations' existence and sustenance possible, their articulations as collectives and what that means for gendered politics in Bangladesh today.

Thinking of these women's organisations as sharing a symbiotic relationship with their inherited field helps us to move away from the arduous process of documenting yet another of chronology of events within women's movements (Azim, 2010; Bano, 2015), resource mobilisation (Nazneen and Sultan, 2009) and charting individuals' prominence within the field (Begum, 1989). Instead, it helps us understand the complicated everyday transactions that take place among the actors—women's organisations, donor agencies, the state and transnational forces—even as their actions contour the field. These women's organisations are in turn part of the larger domain of 'civil society' (including NGOs, INGOs, social movement organisations, faith-based organisations, media, etc.), which is 'that segment of society that interacts with the state, influences the state and yet is distinct from the state' (Chazan, 1992). It has also been conceptualised as the collective/sphere which '(a) locate these struggles;

(b) emphasise the legitimate rights of the people in a democracy to make demands on the state; (c) insist on state accountability and (d) stress the importance of an autonomous site where people can engage in democratic projects for their own sake' (Chandhoke, 2007). Civil society organisations in Bangladesh, like elsewhere in South Asia, are heterogeneous in nature, capturing 'the imagination of both the left and the right' (Chandhoke, 2007) and ranging from 'liberal pluralist, neo-Marxist, and communitarian' (Sahoo, 2013). In spite of its pluralistic nature, the obsession with NGOs within civil society (their terminological differences and ideological inclinations) often flattens the nuanced analysis of 'widely varied functions and forms of organisations' (Fisher, 1997), undermining their complicated transactions with other incumbents in the 'field'. Therefore, I focus on an often ignored but crucial agent within civil society—social movements in general and women's movements in particular.

These transactions are never seamless, nor do they occur among 'equal' parties. The women's organisations (Bangladesh Mahila Parishad, Naripokkho, Women for Women, Ain o Salish Kendra and others) I explore can be understood as embedded within a fragmented, heterogeneous and fluid field, building on the typology that Ray developed based on what she calls the 'distribution of power'[1] and the 'political culture'.[2] There are multiple significant actors inhabiting the field who wield enormous power, both in terms of access to resources and in influence over outcomes. One such 'actor' is the state, the strongest political institution and 'arbiter' of basic human rights. One cannot escape or exist outside the modern state (Schneider and Asad, 2011), and women's organisations in Bangladesh have had no choice but to engage with the legislative state in a dialectical, if not always oppositional, relationship.

Anti-colonialism and the Women's Movement before Partition

The seeds of these women's organisations had been sown long before their formal appearance in the East Pakistani/Bangladeshi political field in the 1970s. The women's movement has always been an integral part of the wider political movements in Bengal, with thousands of women taking part in anti-imperial resistance, independence movements and class or caste-based movements over centuries. The anti-imperial/nationalist movements had multiple ideological influences (Chakravarty, 1980), within which the highly influential Left[3] political parties were more welcoming towards women. As Chakravarty (1980) writes,

> For the first time in the history of India, women stood shoulder to shoulder with men in the fight for freedom. The defiance with which women in their thousands responded to the call for breaking the laws of the satanic government [...] and courting imprisonment on a mass scale, laid the foundation for a dynamic women's movement in this country.

The 1940s in the subcontinent was the age of the Second World War, famine and of independence movements. Women organised themselves in response to these crises, created the Mahila Atma Raksha Samiti (MARS; 'Committee for Women's Self-Defence') and emerged onto the political field in 1943[4] (Das, 2007); by 1947 it had become a mass organisation. In 1945, the All India Women's Congress (AIWC) protested at their situation under colonial rule at the newly founded Women's International Democratic Federation's (WIDF's) convention, formed by 23 war-torn countries to work towards ending any form of war/injustice. MARS became affiliated with them in 1948 (Chakravarty, 1980). The women's movement in the subcontinent had thus managed to establish a global/transnational network from its very inception.

Nationalism and Mobilisation after Partition

After Partition, the influx of Muslim migrants from India combined with the local elites to form the critical mass required for social movements in East Pakistan. Some of them formed neighbourhood women's associations (such as the Gendaria, Wari and Narinda Mahila Samitis), became part of various ladies' clubs as well as women's voluntary associations (Das 2007), aligning either with the Left (that is, towards MARS) or with the state (such as the All Pakistani Women's Association [APWA]). Their paths crossed, but their politics remained very distinct, establishing a pattern that has endured to this day. Women's magazines like *Begum*, *Jayasree* and *Sultana* represented these women; *Begum* critiqued the lack of women's movement in Pakistan, especially in East Pakistan (*Begum*, 1947), and became a platform of protest against polygamy, dowry and inequality in property rights (*Begum*, 1989). These organisations can be considered among the first generation of civil society organisations in East Pakistan, now Bangladesh.

These brave women responded to every national crisis and made their space in history. Muslim women were at the forefront in shielding Hindu families from the violence of the communal riots that followed the declaration of Urdu as the state language in 1948. The Muslim Women's League played a crucial role in unifying women during the Language Movement of 1952, with women leading the processions and demonstrations throughout the country (Das, 1999). The Begum Club[5] aligned itself with the Language Movement. Women held protests, demanding freedom for all political prisoners in 1962 (*Begum*, 2001), and joined other forces in protecting minorities in the aftermath of the riots and ethnic cleansing that engulfed East Pakistan in 1964. Women's associations held public demonstrations during the Indo-Pak War of 1965, and the police attack on a procession of female students on 19 January 1969, was followed by a spontaneous outburst of women revolting against the Ayub Regime, without any political instigation (*Begum*, February 1969). Women made themselves an inevitable part of the nationalist movement by claiming the public space, which paved the way for the women's movements in post-independent Bangladesh.

After Independence: Nation-building and Women's Rights

The nationalist movement for an independent Bangladesh was intertwined with the women's movement from its very inception. The Women's Action Committee led by the East Pakistan Mahila Parishad (EPMP) was born in 1970, with Begum Sufia Kamal[6] as its president and Maleka Begum[7] as its secretary. The EPMP worked to increase women's participation in politics, and organised movements against child marriage and dowry. By March 1971, the EPMP was vocal about the central government's discriminatory attitude towards East Pakistan and, foreseeing the looming catastrophe of war, positioned themselves against the Pakistani state and began to take precautionary measures; these included organising training on first aid and civil defence for women, coordinated by Maleka Khan[8] with the help of the 'Girl Guides'. Meanwhile, members of the EPMP, now the Bangladesh Mahila Parishad (BMP), were introduced to the WIDF representative in India in 1971, who helped them to garner support for the Bangladeshi Liberation War. EPMP leaders toured around India, condemning the mass rape committed by the Pakistani Army as a war crime, and used the trope of human rights violations in speeches, pamphlets and booklets carrying gruesome photos to lay bare the genocide committed by the Pakistani military junta.

My interview with Fauzia Moslem and Maleka Begum in 2014 revealed that many of these activists served in the field hospitals, fought in the war, supported the freedom fighters and helped with the rehabilitation of women who survived the war. Post-independence Bangladesh was a land of revolutionary possibility; and an outburst of feminist energy was channelled towards building a nation of equals. Ayesha Khanam[9] encapsulates the spirit of her time, and the ideology and mass character of the women's movement,

> We envisioned a 'new woman' who would be independent economically and socially, and fight against all forms of oppression.

> Regardless of their political position, progressive women like Sufia Kamal, Nurjahan Murshid, Nilima Ibrahim guided us to establish Bangladesh Mahila Parishad. Although it is true that many of us belonged to Left lineages, it was nevertheless truly an organisation for women's emancipation regardless of their politics. Their gender identity superseded all other forms of identity. (Interview, dated 2 October 2014, Dhaka)

Following the footsteps of the BMP came more organisations and activists. Women for Women (WfW)—a research organisation dealing only with women's issues—was established in 1973, producing knowledge and performing advocacy in order to ensure gender parity in policy-making. The Centre-Left Awami League (AL) established itself as the ruling party after independence, and both the BMP and WfW worked together with AL leaders who were working on women's issues, acting as partners in nation-building. The Bangladesh Constitution ensured gender equality, and women's participation in politics was ensured by reserving seats for women in Parliament. Several pro-women legal reforms took place, and NGOs initiated programmes to empower women at the grassroot level (Begum, 2000, 2002) (Banu, 2012). Prime Minister Sheikh Mujibur Rahman oversaw several rehabilitation programmes for survivors as part of the effort to salvage the war-torn nation, honouring the women who had faced mass rape as 'Birangona' (war-heroines) in order to de-stigmatise them, marrying them off to freedom fighters, or securing jobs (albeit stereotypical: sewing, nursing or that of an office assistant) (Mookherjee, 2008); several prominent activists/revolutionaries (like Maleka Khan, Nilima Ibrahim, Begum Sufia Kamal, Munira Khan and Bela Nabi) worked closely with the state on such programmes.

Autocratic Regimes, Neoliberalism and the Shift to the UN

The assassination of Sheikh Mujibur Rahman in 1975 marked the end of this nation-building alliance. From 1975 to 1990, Bangladesh was ruled by two autocratic regimes. The first, General Ziaur Rahman (Zia)'s regime, oversaw rapid de-nationalisation and economic and trade liberalisation, creating a new entrepreneurial class with vested interests. This neoliberal turn transformed the character of the state, while creating a space for civil society to realign itself. The autocratic regimes coincided with the United Nations 'Decade for Women' (1975–1985), and these regimes upheld the liberal values promulgated under the UN's 'Women in Development' (WID) approach while simultaneously using Islam to legitimise their political positions. Notable developments included the implementation of a 10 per cent quota for women in public and private sector jobs, a separate Ministry for Women's Affairs was established and pressure from the transnational women's movement forced the government to make a separate budget for programmes and research promoting women's empowerment (Kabeer, 1991). At this time, NGOs started to mushroom in order to manage the inflow of aid, and the neoliberal state became a manager of transnational capital flows composed of aid and investments.

The second autocratic regime was led by General Hussain Muhammad Ershad, stretching from Zia's assassination in 1981 to its collapse in 1990. The Ershad regime proved to be the highest recipient of foreign aid since independence, yet, despite investing in several mega-projects, the economy stagnated (Sobhan, 1990). It was in such a political climate that Naripokkho emerged in 1983, established by a group of radical feminists that were mostly trained abroad. Bangladesh had, in the meantime, become one of the signatories of the 1979 UN Convention on the Elimination of all Forms of Discrimination against Women (CEDAW), eventually ratifying CEDAW in 1984 with reservations on Articles 2, 13(a), 16.1(c) and 16.1(f), stating that these 'conflict with *Sharia* law based on Holy Quran and Sunna'.[10] Except for Articles 2 and 16.1(c), reservations were removed from the rest of the articles in 1997. The Ain o Salish Kendra (ASK) was established in 1986—a pioneer in the field of national legal aid and human rights. Resistance against the Ershad regime became pronounced soon after Parliament was dissolved in 1987, and its attempt to stay afloat by pandering to majoritarian Muslim factions further enraged secular Left-Liberal forces, including the women's organisations. The ambivalent position of these autocratic regimes, engaged in a balancing act with both internal pressures and the liberal prerequisites of foreign capital, forced open a space for NGOs, women's organisations and other Left-Liberal and secular forces to thrive. As Naila Kabeer argues, 'Women have been able to capitalize on the *ad hoc* politics of an insecure state' (Kabeer, 1991), in a scenario similar to that which unfolded in Pakistan (Jamal, 2005).[11]

Democratic Regimes, NGO-isation and Administrative Feminism

Ershad's autocratic regime was overthrown in 1990 by a mass uprising led by students, political parties and civil society organisations, and was followed by a series of nominally democratically elected governments. The first was led by the Bangladesh Nationalist Party (BNP) under Khaleda Zia, and the second by a resurgent Awami League under Sheikh Hasina. Free primary and secondary education and a stipend for girls was introduced under the first regime (MoWCA, GOB, 2000), while the National Women's Development Plan was introduced under the second in 1996. Despite some positive changes, women-led regimes did not in general make politics more inclusive. During the 1990s, many movement-based women's organisations had to change their registrations from 'societies' to NGOs in order to receive any foreign grants, coinciding with the requirements of the preparatory committee for the Fourth World Conference on Women in Beijing, 1995. While larger organisations like the BMP, WfW and Naripokkho could mobilise their resources and social networks to retain their radical agendas (Nazneen and Sultan, 2009), smaller organisations became subsumed under the official UN-mandated 'administrative' feminism. NGOs thought to be representatives of civil society became highly politicised, some of them becoming co-opted by the ruling parties (Sabur, 2013a).

Meanwhile, Islamist parties and movements, banned and pushed underground (where they had continued to recruit) by Sheikh Mujib's government, grew in prominence with the Islamic posturing of consecutive autocratic regimes. It was in this context that the formal rehabilitation of anti-liberation forces like the Jamaat-e-Islami and their inclusion in mainstream politics during Zia's regime was a particularly significant development (Sabur, 2013b). Both Islamic and developmental agendas could be reflected in government policy. As Kabeer (1991) suggests, this was because both the Saudi Arabian and the US governments had long-term interests in private capital investments and formed a natural alliance against the Communist bloc. Such a political climate gave rise to fatwa-related violence against women and the demand for Sharia law, which I will be addressing in the next section.

Through all of this, women's organisations continued to fight and negotiate for women's human rights, fuelled by political instability and against the state's indifference. Yet, as the forces that constituted the political field shifted, so did the language of the women's movement. Although Left political parties had been natural allies of the women's movement, conflicts of interest were also equally apparent, magnified by broader geopolitical transformations during the 1960s and 1970s. The EPMP/BMP, for example, despite starting as an affiliate organisation of the Communist Party of Bangladesh (CPB), eventually decided to cut the umbilical cord and became the largest autonomous mass women's organisation in the country, even though many of its members were active members of the CPB or its student wing. Organisations like the BMP, Naripokkho, ASK and, to some extent, WfW may have had different lineages, but all of them shared an ambivalent relationship with the state and political parties. They had to work closely with the state to ensure basic human rights, but retained their dissident voices, especially during the 1980s and 1990s. However, since the 1990s, the political field has been characterised by post-Beijing Declaration repercussions, including NGO-isation, the rise of 'administrative' feminist forces and the deradicalisation of the women's movement.

Defining Women's (Human) Rights through Resistance: Coalitions (1960s–2000s)

Despite its fractured and heterogeneous nature, it was during 1960s–2000s that the women's movement gained the most out of the coalitions that women's organisations managed to establish among themselves and with NGOs, political parties, media and other civil society groups. They deployed discourses related to Violence against Women (VAW), women's legal, political, reproductive and sexual rights, as well as multiple forms of discrimination; all considered legitimate issues within the field. Many of these women's organisations fought hard for equal rights using the existing legal framework offered by CEDAW, making use of what Sara Hussain described as the relevance of the law in terms of 'creating spaces, but also recognition of rights'. Activists like Hussain have been working relentlessly to create such spaces, defining the basic human rights for women through their everyday politics and resistance.

Collective Mobilisation and the Nationalist Turn

We have already seen how transnational collectives consisting of the WIDF, AWIC and EPMP/BMP emerged and mobilised during and after the Liberation War of 1971. Their actions not only defined human rights to a global audience, but also earned international support for the Bangladeshi struggle for independence, especially within the Communist bloc. The BMP's long-term alliances also made them a direct recipient of relief-aid for rehabilitating the war-torn country,[12] and they became the contact point for the global woman's movement in Bangladesh as well as synonymous with progressive movements and the nation-building project. Even though the WIDF disintegrated with the fall of the Communist bloc, after their last convention in Sheffield in 1990, the BMP had managed to realign itself and went on to be part of the UN-led global women's movement.

The senior BMP leadership formed an alliance with Nilima Ibrahim (an AL activist and leader of the Bangladesh Mahila Samity),[13] Maleka Khan and other progressive women activists, and worked closely with the ruling party to establish the Bangladesh Women's Rehabilitation Board in 1972, under which rehabilitation centres provided immediate medical assistance with the help of International Planned Parenthood Federation London and USAID (Banu, 2012). The state, unprepared to deal with mass rape of such magnitude, disciplined these bodies through various medical interventions. The womb became a site of nation-building, where the basic human 'right to live' overpowered the 'will' to retain reproductive rights of the survivors. These events led to two historical steps taken by the state: one, not shaming but acknowledging (to a degree) women's sacrifices in the war, and, two, legalising menstrual regulations (MR), establishing access to abortion before 90 days of pregnancy and going against the prevailing Sharia Law during the time of crisis (Alamgir and D'Costa, 2011).

Coalitions and the Neoliberal Turn

Discourses surrounding the body resurfaced in the post-1975 era as the death toll kept mounting, with dowry-related murders such as that of Saleha Khatun in 1978, the murder of sex workers like that of Shabmeher in 1985, Nurjahan's forced suicide in 1993 after being publicly stoned as per a fatwa that declared her guilty of 'adultery', the death of domestic worker Yasmin under police custody in 1995 and an alarming increase in the number of acid-attack victims. Multiple coalitions emerged out of the resistance to such violence, opening up the space for newer discourses and advocating for new policies and legal frameworks. These coalitions were most effective in the 1980s and 1990s, especially during the autocratic regimes and interim governments; indeed, the kinds of legal and policy reforms that were possible during these regimes became almost impossible under democratic governments. In the following section, we turn to discuss the factors that pulled the various women's organisations together into coalitions and alliances, as well as the forces that created divisions.

Anti-dowry legislation was one of the 16 demands placed by the BMP to the president of the newly independent Bangladesh (*Begum*, 2006); Saleha Khatun's death in 1978 added fuel to this movement. Veteran politician and Member of Parliament Doulotunnesa Khatun (BNP) placed a parliamentary bill before the cabinet, after it was discussed and vetted by the selection committee led by Begum Sufia Kamal (representing BMP) and other civil society representatives, and the Dowry Prohibition Act was passed in 1980 (Banu, 2012). Both Ayesha Khanam and Maleka Begum in their interviews with the author reflected on how these landmark laws could be passed under the autocratic regimes, attributing their success to the fact that MPs were willing to push for the cause and work closely with the women's organisations, rising above their political posturing. The anti-dowry bill opened the path to fight for a Uniform Family Code (UFC) that would ensure equal rights for women in the personal sphere across religious and ethnic divides. Both the BMP and ASK worked closely for years to draft the code; BMP collated the first draft of UFC in 1989 and presented it to civil society organisations in 1992 (BMP, 2006), but it was not formally implemented due to resistance from various religious groups.

Shabmeher's murder in 1985 enraged women's organisations; subsequently, various women's and civil society organisations came together under the BMP's initiative to form the 'Naree Nirjaton Protirodh Committee' ('Violence Against Women Resistance Committee') in 1985. Their core demand was that CEDAW be implemented without any reservations (*Begum*, 2001). They upheld the slogan 'Women's Right Is Human Right' while mobilising for the

UFC. The Ershad regime, however, opted for a quick fix and set up the Family Courts in 1985 for faster trials. While this was a considerable accomplishment, old religious legal frameworks remained the guiding principles of these courts and limited their efficacy. The BMP went on to lead a coalition of 17 organisations under the banner of 'Oikkyobodhdho Nari Samaj' ('United Women's Society')[14] in 1987. They published a 17-point charter to establish women's human rights, with demands including family law reform, increasing the percentage of quotas reserved for women and indigenous people in government jobs, ensuring a minimum wage and equal pay for women in the readymade garment sector, direct elections for reserved seats for women in Union Councils and in the Parliament, among many others (*Begum,* 2001).

The Ershad regime's pandering to Islamist sentiments and forces has already been mentioned, and the declaration of Islam as the state religion in 1988 through the 8th Constitutional Amendment predictably enraged the women's organisations as well as other members of the civil society (including veteran freedom fighters, prominent artists and intellectuals), who stood against this amendment in fear of losing one of the 'four pillars' of the nation-state: secularism. The Oikkyobodhdho Nari Samaj along with the student wings of various political parties held demonstrations all over Bangladesh. Soon this coalition became a platform for resistance against the autocratic regime. In July 1988, Naripokkho petitioned a writ in the court against the 8th Amendment 'stating that this amendment was contrary to the spirit of the constitution, and would work against the establishment of the equality of rights of its citizens' (Azim, 2010). Both fatwa decrees and mobilisation for Sharia Courts grew significantly within a political climate increasingly tolerant of Islamist discourses. Nurjahan's public stoning and subsequent suicide after being condemned for adultery by a fatwa created a massive uproar. Hameeda Hossain depicts the dynamics between locals and activists in women's organisations resisting fatwas at the time:

> In fact, in 1993 when Nurjahan was forced to commit suicide, Mahila Parishad members started the case and following that the other organizations got to act. That became a big movement against fatwa. So, unless you have that supportive role, I think it's difficult for just local groups to respond. (Discussion in workshop on 'Civil Society, Human Rights and Social Justice in Bangladesh', dated 30 August 2018)

Fatwas became endemic during the 1990s, with writers and intellectuals like Taslima Nasrin and Sufia Kamal being identified as *murtad* (apostate) and NGO-workers as infidels. This secular-Islamist contestation has remained a fraught and violent terrain for the women's movement through to the present day.

The 1990s remained politically very volatile for the women's movement, but also witnessed the emergence of new discursive spaces. The Shammilito Nari Samaj (Coalition of Women in the Society), one of the strongest coalitions of the time, was formed to protest the 1995 death of the 14-year-old Yasmin under police custody in Dinajpur, amidst local mass uprisings against the perpetrators (members of the police force) as well as against the ruling BNP regime. Men and women from civil society organisations, journalists, cultural activists and members of political parties (especially from the Left) were mobilised and joined the protests along with the locals, with coalitions of NGOs and women's organisations on the Beijing preparatory committee playing a crucial role in the mobilisations. Members of the coalition protested in the open forum in the Beijing conference in 1995 and presented Yasmin's case as one of violence against women under state patronage. Needless to say, government representatives identified the BMP and WfW as anti-state actors (*Begum*, 2001).

New coalitions were formed among Naripokkho and partner organisations to protect sex workers, in the wake of the evictions from the Kandupatti brothel in Old Dhaka in 1997. Naripokkho reached out to the sex workers protesting the illegal eviction under the banner of Patita Shangram Parishad, and supported them in forming their own organization—Ulka (meteor) (Azim, 2002). Later, 86 organisations dealing with human rights formed a coalition named Shanghati (Solidarity), helping sex workers manoeuvre to fight for their rights (Banu, 2012). By 2000, this coalition had succeeded in getting a ruling from the High Court against the eviction, sex work became recognised as professional work and sex-workers were given the legal right to vote. Firdous Azim argues that these movements expanded the horizons of feminist activism and the meaning of an inclusive citizenry:

> We didn't have the vocabulary, but the sex workers' movement made it very easy then for women's groups, and later, for groups that joined this and other gendered rights groups which then emerged and transformed into LGBT groups, etc. to talk about the issue of sexuality and rights. So, these intersectional involvements provided a new platform and new ways of thinking […] this whole issue of what groups like us do, are we intermediaries, are we buffers, do we work with or do we work on behalf, fluctuates. (Discussion in workshop on 'Civil Society, Human Rights and Social Justice in Bangladesh', dated 30 August 2018)

It should also be noted that this movement had wider equality and human rights implications, for it gradually opened up the space for male and transgendered sex workers and the 'queering' of feminist politics (Azim, 2012).

Two similar coalitions formed with a focus on the 'body' as the site of resistance. The first, the Protirodh (Resistance) network, was formed in 1989 and focused on reproductive health and the state's population-control policy while ensuring the right to access safe birth-control methods; members of the BMP and WfW were also part of this network (Banu, 2012). The second coalition emerged out of resistance against acid violence. Although the BMP and WfW initially worked closely on the matter, the movement was spearheaded by Naripokkho along with ActionAid and BRAC, mobilising their personal networks and securing international funds. The 'Acid

Survivors Foundation' was finally born in 1999, and anti-acid violence legislation was passed in 2002. The biggest accomplishment of this movement was to replace the discourse of 'victimhood' with 'survivors', claiming visibility and the strength to exist in public spaces (Chowdhury, 2011).

By all accounts, the women's organisations explored here lived their radical moments during 1980s and 1990s. The movements were ideologically led, militant in nature, with mass engagement and support by the mainstream media. These coalitions were very effective indeed at reforming laws and producing structural changes, both recognising and defending human rights through their actions. Yet, by the late 1990s, this militant spirit had started to wane, and today women's movement organisations are nowhere nearly as effective. ASK's 2019 annual report, for example, revealed that a total of 1,413 women had been subjected to rape that year alone.[15] A similar report by the BMP showed that the number had reached 731 within the first six months of 2019.[16] In 2016, the rape and murder of Sohagi Jahan *Tonu* in Comilla Cantonment created an uproar among civil society organisations, yet failed to culminate into a mass movement similar to the one surrounding Yasmin's, even though 68 women's organisations, NGOs and civil society bodies have continued their struggle as a coalition under the banner 'Social Resistance Committee' since 2000. Similarly, Hefazat-e-Islam's (HI) grand rally on 6 April 2013, where they presented their 13-point demands, was considered by many to be 'anti-women'.[17] Lamentably, the resistance failed to gain the same currency as that of the anti-fatwa movement of 1990s, with protests against the HI's demands appearing to be the end in itself.[18] Part of this 'deradicalisation' can be attributed to the neoliberal regimes and its anti-political machineries against which the women's movement had battled relentlessly. The human rights activist Khushi Kabir compares her past experiences with present-day mobilisations, and discusses some possible reasons for this decline:

> The agency was much stronger [...] I think that distinction between 'for' and 'with' is very important and very often the role of civil society becomes speaking for and 'on behalf', and whether it's the government, whether it's the corporate sector that you are negotiating with; issues of human rights and social /political justice has been taken over by this group of people—intermediate people. A lot of activists, who would be part of the movements, own the movements, I don't find them now. They are missing in the rural areas. It is defined by the globalized corporate culture. (Discussion in workshop on 'Civil Society, Human Rights and Social Justice in Bangladesh', dated 30 August 2018)

Khushi Kabir's concerns echoed among the participants in the workshop. In order to shed some light on the possible causes of such a deradicalisation, I now turn to my own ethnographic work and reflections from the workshop discussions, combined with archival material.

Deradicalising Moments

Contrary to the popular belief, NGO-isation alone did not deradicalise the women's movement in Bangladesh (Sabur, 2013a), nor did the tectonic shifts in the field happen at once. Deradicalisation happened in various phases. My earlier discussion revealed how the political field was contoured by both local and transnational forces. Apart from the ambivalent relationship of women's organisations with the state, the global effects of Cold War politics, the fall of the Communist bloc, US–Saudi infiltrations, neoliberal reforms, the expansion of the development sector and the mushrooming of NGOs were all factors that were involved in deradicalising the women's movements and the relationships among the agents embedded within the field.

It is necessary to acknowledge how our liberatory dreams during the anti-colonial and nationalist movements were, to a significant degree, fuelled by Left imaginations, bringing women to the centre of the struggle. Women in the newly independent Bangladesh claimed their space as equal citizens in both the private and the public domains. The most radical forces within the women's movement invested their energies in rebuilding the war-torn nation. Working closely with the state to secure women's rights as full citizens put them in an ambivalent position, which led to the first phase of deradicalisation. They were visionaries, but could only be radical within limits for the sake of 'the new women' of a new nation. The BMP's realignment from affiliate to autonomous organisation, distancing itself from its Left lineage, was not a coincidence. Left political parties in Bangladesh dwindled around the 'woman question' and emergent 'identity politics' just like everywhere else in the world. Wendy Brown was right to point out that the growing ritualistic dogmatism of Left parties turned them into one of the most conservative forces in the field, crippled with the dread that identity politics would fragment, if not hijack, their movements, eventually failing to build any coalitions (Brown, 2014); this was true for Bangladesh as well. What is often ignored, however, is the impact of Cold War politics on postcolonial nation states. Bangladesh became a prototypical case where the battle between the Left and neoliberal forces played out and the women's movement bore the brunt, with the assassination of Sheikh Mujibur Rahman in 1975 signifying the fall of the Left and the triumph of neoliberalism.

There were two major shifts in the political field during the subsequent autocratic regimes. First, because most members of civil society and the media were critical of the regimes, and the women's organisations considered democracy as a necessary precondition for women's liberation, the 'enemy' was easily identifiable: the regime and the state itself. We thus witnessed numerous mass mobilisations during this period, holding the state accountable for its failures. Second, these regimes aligned themselves with and gave in to the US–Saudi interests in private capital investment. This alliance inevitably positioned itself against the Communist bloc, and the Bangladeshi state served as a handmaid of these transnational interests, neutering the Left on the ground through imprisonment, extra-judicial killings of activists and the banning of CPB in 1977–1978 (Sarkar, 2015). There were also massive inflows of aid and capital to support development projects during this period, and the neoliberal aspirations of the managerial state were realised. To ensure the flow of aid, the state had to present itself as promoting WID and GAD (Gender and Development) to the UN bodies and donor agencies, leading to women-friendly legislation, effective family court administration, quotas for women in both public and private-sector jobs, women's participation in electoral politics, provisioning contraceptives as part of the population control policy and ensuring 'women's empowerment. NGOs mushroomed to assist the donor agencies along with the state to deliver these services. Unchecked neoliberal development thus led to the second phase of deradicalisation of feminist politics. Women's organisations had no choice but to reckon with the neoliberal forces, replacing Left transnational networks with the UN agencies. Implementing CEDAW and the CSW agenda became the major rallying points for these organisations.

Most of these women's organisations may not be development or service-delivery organisations, but they demanded equal rights and resources for women (Azim, 2010). As the years passed, the demands grew, and new projects required permanent staff, both centrally and regionally. Local needs and the requirements of the 1995 Beijing Platform for Action drove the women's organisations to register as NGOs. Post-Beijing administrative feminism turned many of these organisations into service-delivery organisations, marking the third phase of deradicalisation, whereby, activism was superseded by administration and bureaucracy. As activists observe, most of these organisations spend all their time writing reports for NGO bureaus and donor agencies, grant proposals, coordinating internal meetings with partner organisations; whatever resources are left after this administrative work is spent behind actual activism/movements. This has resulted in the birth of highly professional but exhausted activist feminist subjects[19] who are paid to do the mundane jobs that volunteers do not have the time for.

The Department of Women and Gender Studies at Dhaka University was established in 2000,[20] becoming a breeding ground for development professionals and academics, but not activists. Activists who have been volunteering for years have invested precious capital in the form of 'time'—something that has been hardly recognised in the discourse of the women's movement or how it has shaped the field. The BMP and Naripokkho are membership-based organisations, where the central leadership can effectively balance their profession (day job) and passion (BMP). I argue that time has been and continues to be the single-most important capital, along with their collective social networks consisting of persons they could manoeuvre to set their own agendas, receiving the grants best suited for them, with transnational forces as well as the state having to realign themselves to oblige (Chowdhury, 2005; Nazneen and Sultan, 2009). The trepidation of younger generations is structural, a product of their professions and lifestyle (and even mundane things like time spent commuting or childcare), all factors deterring them from investing as much time as their predecessors, and so from being as effective. Thus, we witness the rise of fierce feminist individuals writing blogs, opening groups discussing feminist issues, engaging in transversal politics, but hardly interested in collectives or willing to join such autonomous women's organisations. For these organisations, the mundane administrative work is crucial for their sustenance, without which the transference of experience-knowledge to succeeding generations or even mobilisation would have been impossible. As Shahzadi Zaman from the BMP articulates:

> It is difficult to sustain a movement. If we want to change things, then enthusiasm needs to be channeled towards back-breaking tedious work like sending mails, organizing meetings, lobbying, and follow-ups. Can we find any alternative which will relieve us from mundane administrative overload? We are stretched; we are tired feminists. The challenge is to sustain the energy after all this and bring about real change. (Discussion in workshop on 'Civil Society, Human Rights and Social Justice in Bangladesh', dated 30 August 2018)

The neoliberal economy nurtured individual entitlement and produced consumerist subject—'empowered' women. It is now possible, at the individual level, to assume the 'activist' role while working for an NGO that promotes gender equality, or a corporation doing CSR (Corporate Social Responsibility) involving women, without being militant—protesting for structural changes. An army of empowered women has thus emerged across classes, but the women's organisations have failed to engage this untapped force to form a 'collective' working towards structural change. The majority of the members of civil society have either consented to the state to fight their battles for them, or have been silenced with the use of coercive force and laws like the Digital Security Act of 2018,[21] losing their critical edge in the process. The media industry has also become extremely corporatised, serving vested interest-groups, while dissident voices have been curbed by imprisoning journalists. Allegiance to the ruling parties has given rise to ineffective/deradicalised movements and a state not susceptible to critique.

Conclusion: In Defence of Women's Organisations

Through our earlier discussions we have witnessed the state becoming more intrusive, if not authoritarian. We have seen how millennial capitalism has debased long-standing democratic institutions, dismantling the infrastructure necessary for delivering justice and shrinking the space for civic engagement. It is in this context that the existence of autonomous organisations has become more important than ever to combine transversal movements with movements for long-term structural changes, both locally and globally. It has become necessary to relive the radical moments, resuscitate the old collectives/coalitions of activists, academics, human rights defenders and practitioners. There are multiple women's/feminist movements active today, but there is no shortcut to tapping the experiences that activists have brought to the field by fusing them with emergent platforms in new media and beyond. These organisations need to reassert their independence, reclaim lost ground, hold the state accountable and make future constructive dialogue between the state and civil society possible. Faced with a new reality where transnational funding is drying up, organisations are bound to reappraise their positions and renew some of the old, effective tools. Under these circumstances, it is possible to have a feminist construction outside the UN-mandated language and create an inclusive, nurturing civic space through intergenerational and intersectional dialogue. The trepidations of today can only usher in a new era in feminist politics and change the political field once more.

Notes

1. 'By *distribution of power*, I mean the pattern of concentration or dispersal of forces in the field. This pattern determines the degree of access an organisation has to policy decisions, its capacity to implement policies and the availability of allies, factors that analysts have considered important features of an organisation's political opportunity structure' (Ray, 1999, 9–10).
2. 'Political culture' refers to 'the acceptable and legitimate ways of doing politics in a given society, strongly influenced by but not reducible to the complex web of class, gender, race, religion and other relations that order society' (Ray, 1999).
3. The Left in Bangladesh was divided between pro-Moscow and pro-Beijing camps. While the former was affiliated with Indo-Soviet socialist camps fighting for national liberation alongside the Awami League (AL) as part of socialist revolutions worldwide, the latter aligned themselves with pro-Pakistani camps in an unholy trinity composed along superpowers like the United States and China (Sarkar, 2015).
4. The Left movement in the Indian Subcontinent was at its prime from 1942 to 1947, with women like Manikuntala Sen, Juifool (Bose) Roy, Latika Sen, Geeta Roy Chowdhury and Renu Roy (Chakravarty) of the Communist Party and Student Federation leading the movement along

with other women leaders. Among Bengali Muslim women, Jobeda Khatun, Begum Shamsunnahar Mahmud and others were part of this committee.

5. *Begum* was one of the first women's weekly magazines, published by women (editors and writers), catering to predominantly Muslim women; it was first published in Kolkata on 20 July 1947.

   In 1954, Mohammad Nasiruddin opened the Begum Club at the office of the journal to provide a forum for women, especially women writers, to discuss different literary issues. The forum's first president was Shamsunnahar Mahmud, and the secretary was Nurjahan Begum. At the beginning, the writers would meet once a month, and later once a year. It was active until 1970. (https://www.thedailystar.net/star-weekend/spotlight/begum-how-one-magazine-began-revolution-1226470 [accessed on 31 May 2020])
6. Begum Sufia Kamal (1911–1999) was a renowned poet and an activist. She was one of the key figures in the nationalist movements and a prominent member of the civil society in independent Bangladesh.
7. Maleka Begum (1944) is a writer and a feminist. She was closely associated with the Chhatro Union (student wing of the Communist Party of East Pakistan/Bangladesh) before she became the general secretary of Bangladesh Mahila Parishad.
8. Maleka Khan was the secretary for the East Pakistan Girl Guides Association. She used her skills to train young women during the war. She also volunteered in the Sufia Kamal-led rehabilitation center for women ravaged by the war.
9. Ayesha Khanam is the president of Bangladesh Mahila Parishad. She was a prominent student leader and a key organiser for the BMP.
10. https://www.thedailystar.net/star-weekend/news/cedaw-dead-end-bangladesh-1711840 (accessed on 31 May 2020).
11. Amina Jamal highlights Women's Action Forum's (WAF) resistance against ppression of General Zia and state-sponsored Islamisation by challenging *Hudood Law* from the 1980s to the 1990s, and what kind of impact it had on women's political and social life.
12. In 1972, Maleka Begum along with Sufia Kamal went to the WIDF Convention in Bulgaria to receive their membership on behalf of the BMP. Bela Nabi (P55, 2010) in her memoire fondly remembers the

East German Cargo flight filled with relief, which was sent for the BMP directly, which they later handed over to the government for distribution, the latter reallocating the BMP's share to redistribute.

13. Bangladesh Mahila Samity built upon the structure left by APWA, sharing similar characteristics and directly patronised by the ruling party.
14. The 17 organisations are: 1. Bangladesh Mahila Parishad, 2. Dhaka Business and Professional Women's Club, 3. Bangladesh Lekhika Shongho (Bangldesh Women Writers' Forum), 4. Women for Women, 5. Federation of Business and Professional Women's Club, Dhaka, 6. Socialist Women's Forum, 7. Bangladesh Naree Mukti Shongshod (Bangladesh Women's Liberation Assembly), 8. Bangladesh Naree Shamiti (Bangladesh Women's Association), 9. Bangladesh Women's Right Movement, 10. Democratic Women's Movements, 11. National Women's League, 12. Women's Labour Committee, 13. Shaptagram, 14. Soroptimist International Club, 15. Bangladesh National Woman Lawyer's Association (BNWLA), 16. Bangladesh Democratic Women's Association and 17. Banani Lion's Club (Begum, 2001).
15. https://www.thedailystar.net/country/rape-victims-doubled-in-2019-in-bangladesh-1847710 (accessed on 31 May 2020).
16. https://www.thedailystar.net/country/731-women-raped-in-bangladesh-in-6-months-1768477 (accessed on 31 May 2020).
17. Hefazat-e-Islam called out key organisers of the Shahabag movement as 'atheists', demanded punishment for their 'blasphemous acts', condemned women's presence/free-mixing in the movement, criticised women for their attires as well as the presence of NGOs, among other things. https://www.bbc.com/news/world-asia-22424708 (accessed on 31 May 2020).
18. https://alalodulal.org/2013/05/28/ngoization/ (accessed on 31 May 2020).
19. Srila Roy identifies the embeddedness of these 'activist subjects' as a political possibility; their hybrid nature of passionate yet professional feminist self can offer the feminist movements the much required impulse (Roy, 2015).
20. The department received the fund from 2005 to 2009 from ISS, Netherlands. https://www.du.ac.bd/academic/department_item/WOS. (accessed on 31 May 2020).

21. https://www.amnesty.org/en/latest/news/2018/09/bangladesh-new-digital-security-act-imposes-dangerous-restrictions-on-freedom-of-expression/ (accessed on 31 May 2020).

References

Alamgir, J. and B. D'Costa. 2011. 'The 1971 Genocide: War Crimes and Political Crimes'. *Economic and Political Weekly*, 46(13): 38–41.

Azim, F. 2002. 'Women and Freedom'. *Inter-Asia Cultural Studies*, 3(3): 347–360.

______. 2010. 'Formulating an Agenda for the Women's Movement: A Review of Naripokkho'. *Inter-Asia Cultural Studies*, 2(3): 389–394.

______. 2012. 'Keeping Sexuality on the Agenda: The Sex Worker's Movement in Bangladesh'. In *South Asian Feminisms*, edited by A. Loomba and R.A. Lukose, 276–284. New Delhi: Zubaan.

Banu, A. 2012. *Feminism in Bangladesh: 1971–2000 Voices from Women's Movement*. Dhaka University.

______. 2015. 'Global-Local Interactions: First Three Decades of the Women's Movement in Bangladesh'. *Journal of the Asiatic Society of Bangladesh* (Hum.), 60(2): 203–230.

Begum, M. 1989. *Banglar Nari Andolon [The Women's Movement of Bengal]*. Dhaka: The University Press Limited.

______. 2001. *Ami Naree: Tinshow Bochorer (Athero-Bish Shotok) Bangali Nareer Itihash (I Am the Woman: Three Hundred Years' History of Bengali Women)*. Dhaka: The University Press Limited.

Bourdieu, P. 2002. *Distinction: A Social Critique of the Judgment of Taste*. London: Routledge.

Brown, W. 2014. 'Resisting Left Melancholy'. *Boundary 2*, 26(3): 19–27.

Chakravarty, R. 1980. *Communists in Indian Women's Movement (1940–50)*. New Delhi: Peoples Publishing House.

Chandhoke, N. 2007. 'Civil Society'. *Development in Practice*, 17(4–5): 607–614.

Chazan, N. 1992. 'Africa's Democratic Challenge'. *World Policy*, 9(2): 279–307.

Chowdhury, E.H. 2005. 'Feminist Negotiations: Contesting Narratives of the Campaign against Acid Violence in Bangladesh'. *Meridians: Feminism, Race, Transnationalism*, 6(1): 163–192.

Chowdhury, E.H. 2011. *Transnationalism Reversed: Women Organizing against Gendered Violence in Bangladesh.* New York: SUNY Press.

Das, H. 1999. *Naree Andolon O Communist Partyr Bhumika (Women's Movement and the Role of Communist Party).* Dhaka: Jatiyo Shahityo Prakash.

_______. 2007. *Smriti Moy Dinguli (Memorable Days).* Dhaka: Jatiyo Shahityo Prakash.

Fisher, W.F. 1997. 'Doing Good? The Politics and Antipolitics of NGO Practices'. *Annual Review of Anthropology*, 26(1): 439–464.

Jamal, A. 2005. 'Transnational Feminism as Critical Practice: A Reading of Feminist Discourses in Pakistan'. *Meridians: Feminism, Race, Transnationalism*, 5(2): 57–82.

Kabeer, N. 1991. 'The Quest for National Identity: Women, Islam and the State in Bangladesh'. *Feminist Review*, 37(1): 38–58.

Mookherjee, N. 2008. 'Gendered Embodiments : Mapping the Body-Politic of the Raped Woman and the Nation in Bangladesh'. *Feminist Review*, 88: 36–53.

Nazneen, S. and M. Sultan. 2009. 'Struggling for Survival and Autonomy: Impact of NGO-ization on Women's Organisations in Bangladesh'. *Development*, 52(2): 193–199.

Ray, R. 1999. *Fields of Protest: Women's Movements in India*. Minnesota: University of Minnesota Press.

Roy, S. 2015. 'New Activist Subjects: The Changing Feminist Field of Kolkata, India'. *Feminist Studies*, 40(3): 628–656.

Sabur, S. 2013a. 'Did "NGOization" Deradicalize the Women's Movement? Alal of Dulala'. Available at http://alalodulal.org/2013/05/28/ngoization/%0Ae (accessed on 31 May 2020).

_______. 2013b. 'Post Card from Shahabag'. *International Sociological Association (ISA) e-Symposium*, March: 1–17.

Sahoo, S. 2013. *Civil Society and Democratization in India: Institutions, Ideologies and Interests*. New York: Routledge.

Sarkar, S. 2015. 'The Role of the Left in Bangladesh's Democracy: Challenges and Prospects'. In *Democratic Goverance and Politics of the Left in South Asia,* edited by S. Dasgupta, 228–244, New Delhi: Aakar Books.

Schneider, N. and T. Asad. 2011. 'The Suspicious Revolution: An Interview with Talal Asad'. *The Immanent Frame*. Available at http://blogs.ssrc.

org/tif/2011/08/03/the-suspicious-revolution-interview-with-talal-asad/ (accessed on 15 July 2015).

Sobhan, R. 1991. *The Decade of Stagnation: The State of the Bangladesh Economy in the Late 1980s*. Dhaka: The University Press Limited.

Interviews and Discussions

Ayesha Khanam, Interview dated 2 October 2014, Dhaka.

Firdous Azim, Discussion in workshop on 'Civil Society, Human Rights and Social Justice in Bangladesh', dated 30 August 2018.

Hameeda Hossain, Discussion in workshop on 'Civil Society, Human Rights and Social Justice in Bangladesh', dated 30 August 2018.

Khushi Kabir, Discussion in workshop on 'Civil Society, Human Rights and Social Justice in Bangladesh', dated 30 August 2018.

Shahzadi Zaman, Discussion in workshop on 'Civil Society, Human Rights and Social Justice in Bangladesh', dated 30 August 2018.

3

Political Failure and the Suffering of Stateless 'Non-Citizens': Civil Society Perspectives on the Rohingya Crisis

Paul Chaney

This chapter explores the crisis facing an estimated 900,000 Rohingya people (United Nations, 2018), a Muslim minority group (a variation of the Sunni religion) that has fled persecution in the western state of Rakhine, Myanmar. The Rohingyas have sought sanctuary in the south-eastern district of Cox's Bazar in Bangladesh. They are a stateless people regarded as 'non-citizens' by both Myanmar and Bangladesh, and are subject to inhuman treatment, oppression and rights denial. In this chapter, attention centres on the 'situated knowledge' expressed in civil society accounts of the emergency; specifically, the perspectives of non-governmental organisations (NGOs) working with the Rohingya refugees. The analysis is based on a range of primary and secondary sources—including the views of Rohingya representatives and NGOs (alternatively, civil society organisations or CSOs) gathered during research workshops—as well as NGOs' data submitted to the 2018 third cycle United Nations' Universal Periodic Review (UPR), the official monitoring mechanism associated with UN human rights treaties.

Whilst the Government of Bangladesh espouses a participatory approach to its rights obligations (for example, 'Bangladesh will … continue to fully involve CSOs in promoting human rights at all levels', Government of Bangladesh 2013, 18), the following discussion provides insight into the balance of rhetoric versus reality. It reveals how the official Government of Bangladesh's response to the crisis is failing to address a broad range of rights violations including: access to health care, violence, intimidation and sex trafficking. Some groups within the refugee population fare particularly badly, notably women, girls and disabled people. This chapter argues that government must end its mistrust and growing repression of civil society and engage with NGOs and, in particular, Rohingya people, in order to shape an effective crisis response that ends their inhumane treatment.

Context

Over the past century, there has been a regular influx of Rohingya refugees into Bangladesh. They fled Myanmar in the face of violent military repression, Buddhist extremism and ethnic discrimination. Hitherto, for around a thousand years, they resided in Arakan (Ahmed, 2010). Following invasion by the Rakhine, this independent kingdom became a part of Burma in 1785. The indigenous people of Arakan were predominantly Hindus and Muslims. The Rakhine referred to the Rohingyas as kula or 'dark-skinned people' (Ware and Laoutides, 2018). In the face of discrimination, they took flight to northern Arakan in today's Myanmar and have become known as Rohingya. In the wake of this migration, the Rakhine and Rohingya co-existed but ethnic tensions flared-up during the British-colonial era. These continued over the ensuing decades, leading to a gradual Rohingya exodus from Myanmar to Bangladesh in the 1970s. A key point was reached in 1982 when the Burmese government stripped the Rohingya people of their citizenship; the administrative pretext of the ruling elite was that this was because they were not able to prove that their ancestors had settled in Burma before 1823 (Kyaw, 2017).

Military operations in Myanmar saw a further exodus of 260,000 Rohingyas to Bangladesh during 1991–1992. Ongoing oppression resulted in another crisis point in 2017. As a UN account explained:

'The cornerstone of the oppression is lack of legal status. Successive laws and policies regulating citizenship and political rights have become increasingly exclusionary in their formulation, and arbitrary and discriminatory in their application' (UNHRC, 2018). This prompted 'armed attacks by a Rohingya group, the Arakan Rohingya Salvation Army, against more than 20 Myanmar police stations and an army base on 25 August 2017. As Ahsan (2018) explains, 'the violence it let loose was precipitated by a continuing campaign of atrocities by the Myanmar authorities against the Rohingyas'. The Myanmar Armed Forces responded to these attacks with a 'widespread assault, ostensibly against the Rohingya armed group which they deem a terrorist organisation, but now demonstrably also against the civilian population of the region' (Beyrer and Kamarulzaman, 2017). According to one account, 'violence was the direct cause of death for at least 6,700 Rohingya civilians, including 730 children, living in the state of Rakhine, Myanmar, in the initial 31 days following the latest upsurge of unrest [in…] 2017' (Friedrich, 2018). In consequence, hundreds of thousands fled across the Bangladesh border.

One CSO described the situation as the refugees reached Cox's Bazaar:

> … Pre-existing settlements have effectively merged into one densely populated mega-settlement of more than half a million people, who are crammed along a narrow peninsula trying to find what shelter they can. It is essentially a massive rural slum—and one of the worst slums imaginable. There are hardly any latrines so people have tried to rig up their own plastic sheeting around four bamboo poles, but there is nowhere for their waste to go except into the stream below. That is the same stream that, just 10 miles away, others are using to collect drinking water. This has all the makings of a public health emergency. (White, 2017)

According to another report, 'Overall, the living conditions of Rohingya refugees inside the overcrowded camps remain dismal. Mental health is poor, proper hygiene conditions are lacking, malnutrition is endemic, and physical/sexual abuse is high' (Milton et al., 2017). The official response to the unfolding crisis has been too limited and too late. Writing a year after the mass exodus another civil society account concluded: 'It is unacceptable that watery diarrhoea remains one of the biggest health issues we see in the camps. The infrastructure to meet even the most basic needs of the population is still not in place' (Murphy, 2018).

The trauma of the hazardous border crossing combined with decades of oppression has left its mark on the health of the refugees. Recent studies underline their vulnerability. One found that '36 per cent of its participants had Post Traumatic Stress Disorder symptoms while 89 per cent had depression symptoms' (Wali et al., 2018). Another stated that, 'Even using conservative projections of somewhere between 15 to 18 per cent would place the likely number of Rohingya living with a disability in Bangladeshi displacement camps between 130,000 and 180,000 people' (Landry and Tupetz, 2018). However, the troubling reality is that 'the needs of persons with disabilities and older persons are not sufficiently being taken into account in the [emergency] response ... the challenge is really about the NGOs' financial ability to deliver programming to meet enormous disability needs. Moreover, humanitarian funding agencies rarely prioritize disability before, during, or after complex emergencies' (Arbeiter Samariter-Bund et al., 2017).

NGOs' Perspectives on the Crisis

We now consider civil society perspectives on the Rohingya crisis; the discussion is organised around a series of thematic sub-headings.

Gender-based Oppression and Discrimination

This manifests itself in violence, trafficking and sexual exploitation and constitutes a clear violation of Bangladesh's obligations under Article 6 of the United Nations Convention on the Elimination of All

Forms of Discrimination against Women (CEDAW, ratified in 1984).[1] As one CSO put it, we need to improve the 'protection of vulnerable Rohingya refugees to ensure protection measures are in place to protect vulnerable Rohingya refugee children and women from sexual exploitation and violence' (Aparajeyo Bangladesh, 2017). Another alluded to the 'continuous vulnerability of the Rohingya, being subject to human trafficking and smuggling under harsh conditions on boats to other countries in the region' (Institute on Statelessness and Inclusion, 2017). Others spoke of how children, along with young women, have a particularly high risk of becoming victims of trafficking and organ trading (Solidarity Group on Bangladesh, 2017) and called on government to take measures to protect the vulnerable Rohingya refugee women and children from being trafficked and provide them with care and relief as well as rehabilitation. Earlier accounts point to the complicity of the authorities in these violations. According to one, 'Local people, police, and security forces use this space of vulnerability to their own advantage and are frequently reported as raping Rohingya girls during raids and forced repatriations' (Uddin 2015).

Other civil society voices alluded to a lack of political will and government's failure to act on earlier UN recommendations. A typical demand was that the government should implement recommendations accepted at the last UPR (circa 2012) to address violent acts of religious intolerance, discrimination and gender-based violence (Christian Solidarity Worldwide, 2017). Recent studies concur and underline the precarious position of women. One analysis of gender norms and freedom of movement found that in the refugee camps 24 and 35 per cent of married and unmarried women, respectively, said that they could never go alone to the local market (MSNA/ISCG, 2019). As the following outlines, this is just one aspect of the inequalities that women and girls face:

> As refugees, they are not allowed to find employment in Bangladesh. At the same time, state support is minimal, and so they have to eke out a living from whatever work is available. The mobility of refugee

> men is highly restricted by violence and intimidation, which forces refugee women into the role of the family's breadwinner. Despite this, the women's status has not improved in either the family or the community. On the contrary, the women are exposed to increased violence from their families, the refugee community and outsiders. Though all refugees suffer violence, women face it both inside and outside the home. Their political status as refugees and a lack of community support in the camps combine to increase their vulnerability. (Akhter and Kusakabe, 2014)

Legal and International Treaty Failings

A key problem adding to the crisis is the fact that Bangladesh lacks any domestic laws guaranteeing the protection of stateless and refugee population (Yesmin, 2016). This is compounded by the country's failure to sign key international treaties and respond to the UN's recommendations dating back as far as the First Cycle UPR in 2008. The latter stated:

> … The lack of a legal framework to deal with refugees further provides for an *ad hoc* environment of cooperation with Government institutions which in turn provide an insecure and unpredictable protection environment for refugees…. There are a large number of refugees in Bangladesh without access to asylum procedures and refugee status determination. It is recommended that Bangladesh recognizes the non-registered Rohingya population from the Northern Rakhine State in Myanmar as refugees on a *prima facie* basis and that Bangladesh establish asylum and refugee status determination procedures. (United Nations Human Rights Council Working Group on the Universal Periodic Review, 2008, 21)

Twelve years on, there has been no progress and the civil society discourse continues to urge government to accede to and fully implement the 1954 and 1961 Statelessness Conventions and the Refugee Convention (1951) in order to protect all stateless Rohingya refugees on the Bangladeshi territory, by seeking the cooperation of the international community with sustainable integration efforts and through negotiating resettlement programmes with third countries (Institute on Statelessness and Inclusion, 2017). Here the core message is to, '... ensure that those claiming asylum are able to access refugee status determination procedures without discrimination of any kind' (Amnesty International, 2018).

The Right to Nationality

A further trope in the civil society discourse is to ensure that all children born in the territory of Bangladesh, or to a Bangladeshi parent, are guaranteed without discrimination their right to a nationality (Institute on Statelessness and Inclusion, 2017). The current failure of Bangladesh to grant citizenship rights is a breach of the country's obligations under Article 7 of the UN Convention on the Rights of the Child ('the child shall be registered immediately after birth and shall have the right from birth to a name, the right to acquire a nationality ...') (Chaney, 2018).[2] In consequence, CSOs are calling for legal reform, in order to 'address all concerns related to the right to nationality, statelessness and discrimination in the draft citizenship bill, and produce a new draft citizenship bill (Abrar, 2016, unpaginated), which complies with relevant international standards and allows for considered public debate and consultation' (Institute on Statelessness and Inclusion, 2017).

Suppression of Civil Society and Intimidation of Human Rights Defenders

In its Second Cycle UPR Report of 2012 the UN called on the government to allow NGOs to carry out their work regarding refugees and also to increase its efforts to ensure that human rights defenders are protected and allowed to conduct their work without hindrance, intimidation or harassment both at the national and local level (UNHRC, 2012). In its submission to the Third Cycle UPR, the government claimed 'Bangladesh will ... continue to fully involve

CSOs in promoting human rights at all levels' (Government of Bangladesh, 2013). Yet, over recent years, the political context for CSOs in Bangladesh has deteriorated and the rights agenda has been pushed into the background. In consequence, there is shrinking political space for civil society (Saidul Islam, 2011; Mohajan, 2014; Suykens, 2018; Chowdhury, Jahan and Rahman, 2017). For its part, the ruling administration also claimed in its UPR submission that it 'is providing full access to all international partners and agencies including UN, INGOs, humanitarian actors, media and other civil society organizations to work in Cox's Bazar and support the Rohingyas' (Government of Bangladesh, 2018, p. 19, paragraph 129). Contesting this claim, the UN Human Rights Committee has registered its concern about limitations on the rights to freedom of opinion, expression and association, as well as intimidation and harassment of journalists, bloggers and human rights defenders (HRC, 2018). This anxiety is echoed in the civil society discourse. For example, as one CSO asserted, the government should 'end any formal and informal restrictions preventing the UN and NGOs from providing aid to refugees' (Amnesty International, 2018).

The plight of Human Rights Defenders (HRDs) is a particular concern. For example, one CSO account reported how, on 7 September 2017, Burmese photojournalists Minzayar Oo and Hkun Lat were arrested by the police in Cox's Bazar whilst they were documenting the dismal conditions in which hundreds of thousand Rohingyas lived after they fled violence in Rakhine state. The journalists were taken to Dhaka for interrogation and accused of breaching immigration laws and gathering secret information. A court granted them bail on 23 September 2017 but the charges have not been dropped. As the CSO noted,

> This arrest [has] had a chilling effect on HRDs documenting the situation of Rohingya refugees and caused a certain amount of self-censorship on the issue. Bangladeshi authorities also issued regulations forbidding people to transport or shelter migrants, which puts HRDs and NGOs at risk of judicial harassment. (Front Line Defenders, 2017)

Forced 'Repatriation'

In its submission to the UPR, the Government of Bangladesh claimed that it supported the Rohingyas' 'right to safe, dignified, voluntary return to their homes in Myanmar [based on] ... voluntariness, non-criminalization, livelihood, resettlement, reintegration and other universal elements of human rights' (Government of Bangladesh, 2018). However, a significant strand of the civil society UPR discourse is critical of its record on repatriation. Thus, for example, one CSO referred to how 'the government's inconsistent response to the influx over the last year has at times compounded difficulties for refugees fleeing violence. Following the violence in October 2016, the Border Guards were instructed to push Rohingya refugees back across the border (reinforcing a long standing and unlawful policy)' (Amnesty International, 2018). The latter being a clear violation of Article 13 rights in the International Covenant on Civil and Political Rights (ICCPR).[3]

Others have also been highly critical of the government. For example, one CSO said that the government 'should respect the Principle of non-refoulement, ensure an effective resettlement programme for Rohingya *refugees* and improve access to aid and shelter' (Christian Solidarity Worldwide, 2017). Another condemned Bangladesh's call for Rohingya refugees to be returned to Myanmar and the signing of a repatriation agreement between the two countries (Institute on Statelessness and Inclusion, 2017). In a further observation, an NGO asserted,

> We remain concerned, however, that a joint working group, established by the governments of Bangladesh and Myanmar to discuss the repatriation of Rohingya refugees, may not be sufficiently robust to ensure full respect for the human rights of the Rohingya, including to refugee status in accordance with international law or a safe, voluntary and dignified return to their homes. (Amnesty International, 2018, 6)

As a result of these concerns, refugees have demanded that Myanmar guarantee their safety and freedom of movement, as well as citizenship before any potential return can take place. They also demand that UN peacekeeping forces be deployed in Rakhine, and that the military personnel who carried out the 2017 massacre face justice. Yet, when the Myanmar government subsequently signed a memorandum of understanding with two UN agencies (UNHCR, 2018) to pave the way for the repatriation of Rohingya refugees, the refugees were not consulted. In consequence, when, in 2019, 3,450 Rohingya families were offered a voluntary return to Rakhine, all declined.

International Treaty Violations

In its UPR submission the Government of Bangladesh claimed that it 'remains sensitized about the rights of the Rohingyas' (Government of Bangladesh, 2018). In legal terms, it is a signatory (c. 1979) to the UN International Convention on the Elimination of All Forms of Racial Discrimination (CERD).[4] The country also has duties under Article 11, 'freedom of movement' in the ICCPR. Yet, a core strand of the civil society discourse refutes any notion that the government is 'sensitized' to Rohingya rights. Instead, it details a series of violations. For example,

> Government has also announced restrictions on inhabitants of the planned settlements. Rohingya are not permitted to leave the camp, including to live with family or friends. They are also barred from travelling by vehicle within the country and landlords are prohibited from renting to them and only those registered as refugees will qualify for official assistance. (Amnesty International, 2018)

Another complained that, 'To date, the Rohingya are deemed "illegal migrants" in Bangladesh, and lack protection and enjoyment of basic rights' (Institute on Statelessness and Inclusion, 2017). Another added, 'It is important that it [Government of Bangladesh] ensures rights, provides access to international humanitarian agencies, and complies with international refugee protection standards. (Human Rights Watch, 2017).

Notwithstanding such criticism, with the passing of time, the government's response is becoming more repressive. Thus, for example, in late 2019, Bangladesh's Parliamentary Standing Committee on Defence recommended that a wall be built around the Cox's Bazar camps. Whilst at the same time the government demanded that the Bangladesh Telecommunication Regulatory Commission order telecommunication operators to shut down mobile phone services in the camps. The civil society response was forthright in highlighting how this would further marginalise and isolate the refugees, stopping them from communicating with their relatives living in Myanmar and other parts of the world, not the least because many Rohingyas rely on remittances sent by their diaspora and usually receive phone calls informing them of the money transfers.

Children's Rights

In the civil society UPR discourse significant attention centred on children's welfare rights. A number of NGOs spoke of the urgent need to provide education for children and

> ensure assistance reaches all vulnerable children in need (newly arrived Rohingya children and those who have been living in Bangladesh before the recent influx), [the official response needs to...] include education in the response plan and reopen existing non-formal schools as soon as possible for their psycho-social healing. (Child Rights Advocacy Coalition in Bangladesh, 2017)

Another account referred to gaps and constraints in the provision of education for bureaucratic reasons as well as cultural attitudes to girls' schooling. The latter refers to social norms which restrict mobility for girls after puberty, as well as concerns over perceived safety threats at learning facilities. Other accounts highlight how low attendance rates at educational facilities affect adolescents aged 12 and over, but particularly adolescent girls.[5] In terms of bureaucratic constraints, 'only the levels 1–11 of the Learning Competency Framework and Approach have been endorsed [by Bangladeshi officials]. The approval of the levels III–IV is still being considered by the Government of Bangladesh' (Inter Sector Coordination Group, 2019).

Other CSO UPR submissions referred to the need to address breaches of Article 24 of the UN Convention on the Rights of the Child ('combating disease and malnutrition …'). For example, 'Children and women suffer from one or more forms of malnutrition including low birth weight, wasting, stunting, being underweight, Vitamin A deficiencies, iodine deficiency disorders and anaemia' (Child Rights Advocacy Coalition in Bangladesh, 2017). The clear message to the authorities is that, 'these children need extra support to ensure their emotional well-being and also to prevent the risks (i.e., malnutrition, diseases, trafficking, violence, etc.) they are exposed to' (Child Rights Advocacy Coalition in Bangladesh, 2017). Recent academic studies support this and outline the severity of the malnutrition problem. For example, Mahmood et al. (2017) observe that,

> in Bangladesh, nearly 20 per cent of Rohingya children suffer from wasting.... Stunting, or low height for age, [this] is caused by chronic malnutrition and exists among 60 per cent of Rohingya child refugees in Bangladesh, a rate 50 per cent higher than the rest of the Bangladesh population (which itself has high rates of malnutrition).

This has led to evidence-based calls for the crisis response to be improved: the 'high prevalence of anaemia and poor dietary diversity highlight the need to provide more diversified family rations, expand supplemental fortified food distributions, and support continued breastfeeding' (Leidman et al., 2018).

Allied to the foregoing, a further trope in the civil society discourse underlines the suffering of Rohingya mothers. For example, one NGO reported:

> There are also many women who have fled Myanmar with their newborns as well as pregnant women who are giving birth in Bangladesh.

> It is feared that many of these babies will perish if no action is urgently taken to ensure access to better hygienic conditions, health care, and adequate shelter. (Solidarity Group for Bangladesh, 2018)

Recent studies concur; for example, one alluded to the fact that,

> 40,000 Rohingya women are estimated to be pregnant, and ensuring emergency obstetric services in the difficult-to-access area is quite challenging and contributes to maternal morbidity and mortality … the services provided during childbirth in the Rohingya community are inadequate. Facility delivery (institutional normal vaginal delivery in the presence of skilled birth attendants) is low, at 22 per cent. (Hasan-Ul-Bari and Ahmed, 2018)

Impact on Local, Indigenous People

A further strand of the civil society discourse focused on the impact of the crisis on local, indigenous people and growing tensions with the refugee population. One CSO account quoted the UN's earlier, 2012 UPR recommendations on this issue. This said that the Government of Bangladesh must 'continue improving the conditions of … indigenous people, refugees and migrants taking into account the special situation and difficulties that those groups have to overcome'. It protested that this recommendation had been ignored (Cultural Survival and American Indian Law Clinic, 2017). Another recalled, 'When indigenous residents complained [of the influx of refugees], there were clashes and the houses of 70 indigenous residents were burnt to the ground' (Amnesty International, 2018). Further accounts reveal the dire impact of the crisis on local people's food security. For example, one alluded to the fact that

> a worsening trend was found for the host communities, which show an increased number of households with poor/borderline food consumption … [presently] only 20 percent of the households are found with an acceptable food consumption. A decreased mobility caused by the monsoons and the impact of the [refugee] influx on

> the labour market represent the main factors behind these negative trends. (World Food Programme, 2018)

As the foregoing suggests, the economic impact on the host communities is a growing problem. This is because many indigenous people have lost access to previously farmed lands (often government forest land) and have simultaneously lost work opportunities to the cheaper refugee labour market. Furthermore, forest products on which local people previously depended are no longer available. As the UN reflected, 'It has also become increasingly clear that the response actors [that is, NGO aid providers] will need to increase their focus on host community food security, particularly in hard-hit communities' (United Nations Office for the Coordination of Humanitarian Affairs, 2019). It also highlighted the impact of the crisis on local education, noting that, 'Bangladeshi para-teachers have left host community schools for higher paid work in the camps learning facilities, increasing student-teacher ratios in the [local, indigenous] schools, and leading to tensions over the impacts of the Rohingya infux' (United Nations Office for the Coordination of Humanitarian Affairs, 2019). Recently, the situation has deteriorated further and the police have accused refugees of trafficking methamphetamine pills from Myanmar. Adding to the malaise, in 2019, a fourth Rohingya refugee was shot dead in the fallout over the murder of local government official Omar Faruk by suspected Rohingya criminals. This led to civil unrest with hundreds of local people blocking the road to a refugee camp, burning tyres and vandalising shops visited by refugees.

For its part, the Bangladeshi government has claimed, 'To maintain security of the Rohingyas, additional police check posts have been established, and more than 1,200 law enforcement officials and 1,700 military personnel have been deployed in Cox's Bazar' (Government of Bangladesh, 2018). Yet, civil society actors' accounts suggest this response is inadequate. They speak of fear and intimidation in the face of the rise of criminal gangs. The problem is compounded by security and law and order personnel leaving the camps each evening so that they are unpoliced overnight. According to CSO reports, community-based security interventions in the camps, including basic requirements such as lighting, and the presence of law enforcement authorities need continuous strengthening.

The extreme impact of the crisis on the environment is also of major concern. As a recent study explained,

> In addition to the humanitarian challenges, the mass influx of Rohingya refugees has resulted in environmental degradation both within the refugee camps and in the surrounding areas. The expansion of existing campsites has led to more than 2,000 hectares of forest loss in the Cox's Bazar region ... the remaining elephant habitat is under severe pressure from uncontrolled fuelwood collection in the forest.... The pressure on forests has caused tensions with local people. (Mukul et al., 2019)

The civil society discourse supports this assessment. It underlines how environmental protection and conservation issues have a direct impact on human security and protection, with a multiplier effect on refugee camps. Thus, the lands in and around the refugee camps are characterised by soil erosion and degradation. This coupled with monsoon rains puts refugees' physical security at risk, especially refugees with specific needs. In criticising the government response another CSO concluded, 'The human right to a healthy natural environment, thus sustaining humanity and life on earth, deserves accurate attention' (Center for Global Non-killing, 2017). By way of further illustration of the increasing repression of civil society, the CSO discourse also expressed 'serious concern over reports of excessive force against environmental defenders as well as harassment and stigmatisation of environmental HRDs by associating their activities with terrorist activities' (International Service for Human Rights, 2017).

Conclusion

A decade ago, an analysis had concluded,

> For Bangladesh, there is an urgent need to create a refugee law that provides work permits, and even short-term dual citizenship to those refugees in the border region. Given its location, resources, and capability, Bangladesh, is in a position to create a refugee policy that will prevent long-term encampment of refugees, militarization of Rohingya camps, and consequently, avert potential conflict behaviour within its borders. (Rahman, 2010)

Instead, as the foregoing analysis reveals, the government response to Rohingya refugees in Bangladesh has concentrated on providing transitory humanitarian relief. Whilst international agencies and NGOs have made great efforts, there has been less state action to improve living conditions in the camps. In essence, the official response continues to be one of containment based on notions of difference rather than the extension of citizenship and long-term integration of refugees into Bangladeshi society. This is vividly illustrated by recent government proposals to relocate 100,000 refugees from Cox's Bazar to Bhasan Char, a diminutive island in the Bay of Bengal. The civil society discourse is unified and unequivocal in its opposition to this idea. For example,

> for the Rohingya, Bangladesh's Bhasan Char will be like a prison … relocating refugees to unsafe island would risk lives and livelihoods … dumping a battered and traumatized people on Bhasan Char to face yet another threat to their survival is not a solution. Bangladesh should terminate the relocation plans. (Adams/HRW, 2019)

Another fact is that the Rohingya crisis cannot be divorced from the wider issue of religious extremism and instability in the region (Chaney and Sahoo, 2020). In part, this has shaped the Government of Bangladesh's flawed response to the crisis. This is because a small minority of Rohingya refugees are involved with Islamic extremists.

They are associated with militant groups such as the Arakan Rohingya Islamic Front, Jamaat-e-Islami, Tehrek-Azadi Arakan, the Rohingya Patriotic Front and Rohingya Solidarity Organisation. All are active in the border area of Myanmar and Bangladesh. Many are pressing for a new mode of citizenship that challenges the established geo-politics of the region, namely, membership of a separate Islamic state. Thus, in part, the Government of Bangladesh's failure to extend citizenship rights to the Rohingya reflects its fear of history repeating itself, for as an earlier study notes, 'One consequence of the Rohingya's influx that struck Bangladesh in 1978 was the destabilization of the government following its inability to cope with the Rohingya intruders or migrants in its border areas' (Naushin Parnini, 2013). Accordingly,

> In public, the Jamaat is keeping a low profile, but that is hardly any reason to suppose it and some other Islamist groups will not mount surreptitious campaigns to recruit young Rohingyas in armed action against the Bangladesh state and government. It is a fear which keeps the Sheikh Hasina government on its toes. (Ahsan, 2018)

As the civil society discourse emphasises, an enduring answer to the Rohingya crisis must include the right to return to Myanmar. This should be a priority for the international community 'in order to avoid repeating the humanitarian crisis.... Efforts to resettle Rohingya must also be continued by the UN's member nations ... the durable solution for the Rohingya crisis lies within Myanmar ... parliament has the opportunity to end an historical suffering' (Mahmood et al., 2017). However, this is a highly unlikely scenario owing to a broad range of factors, including, the ongoing oppression of the Rohingya driven by Buddhist nationalists and the Myanmar military, the stifling of Aung San Suu Kyi and other erstwhile human rights champions and the 2019 failure of governments and international agencies to consult Rohingya people on an initial scheme of voluntary return to Rakhine, thereby, further undermining their trust in government.

By now it should be clear that sole blame for human and citizenship rights violations of the Rohingya over recent years does not lie with the Government of Bangladesh. The Bangladeshi state has been overwhelmed by the crisis and, as a resource-poor country, it is in dire need of greater international support. Contemporary civil society discourse recognises this and includes calls to 'redouble bilateral and multilateral diplomatic efforts through regional and international forums to ensure safe and speedy return of all Rohingya refugees to Myanmar' (Human Rights Forum, Bangladesh, 2017). Such views recognise that the United Nations is not the sole broker and acknowledges the role of the Association of Southeast Asian Nations (ASEAN). Unfortunately, the latter has achieved little success, as an earlier study account explains:

> Attempts by the ASEAN Secretary General to include the Rohingya issue into ASEAN's agenda and efforts within the Intergovernmental Commission on Human Rights (AICHR) to discuss the matter have failed. Together with some ASEAN members, Myanmar opposed these attempts by invoking the principle of non-interference in internal affairs [of ASEAN member states] and the need for consensus in taking up the issue. (Petcharamesree, 2016)

A further obstacle preventing resolution of the crisis is the unwillingness of Russia and China, both members of the UN Security Council, to invoke the legal obligation of the UN Charter and back a demand for Myanmar to allow the Rohingyas to return to their villages be legally recognised as citizens.

All of this means that the plight of the Rohingyas is an increasingly desperate one owing to political failure on the part of the international community and governing elites. It is evidenced by the broad range of rights violations highlighted by CSOs discussed in this chapter. It has been compounded by individual factors such as the Bhasan Char relocation plans, the switching off of telecommunications networks in the refugee camps and Bangladesh's Parliamentary Standing Committee on Defence's recommendation that a wall be built around the Cox's Bazar camps. At the heart of this genocidal malaise is the increasingly repressive stance adopted by the Bangladeshi state; one that is fuelled by its failure to embrace dialogue with NGOs, end rights violations and empower—as well as extend citizenship rights to—the Rohingya people. In the face of this *impasse*, future civil society advocacy and mobilisation is more important than ever.

Notes

1. States Parties shall take all appropriate measures, including legislation, to suppress all forms of traffic in women and exploitation of prostitution of women.
2. Ratified in 1990.
3. An alien lawfully in the territory of a State Party to the present Covenant may be expelled therefrom only in pursuance of a decision reached in accordance with law and shall, except where compelling reasons of national security otherwise require, be allowed to submit the reasons against his expulsion and to have his case reviewed by, and be represented for the purpose before, the competent authority or a person or persons especially designated by the competent authority.
4. *Inter alia*, 'Each State Party undertakes to engage in no act or practice of racial discrimination against persons, groups of persons or institutions and to ensure that all public authorities and public institutions, national and local, shall act in conformity with this obligation'.
5. Around 34 per cent of which attend temporary learning centres compared to 54 per cent of boys, MSNA/ ISCG 2019, 23.

References

Abrar, C.R. 2016. 'The Curious Contents of the Citizenship Law'. Available at https://www.thedailystar.net/op-ed/politics/the-curious-contents-the-citizenship-law-1233943 (accessed on 22 November 2019).

Adams, B. 2019. 'For Rohingya, Bangladesh's Bhasan Char "Will Be Like a Prison'. Available at https://www.hrw.org/news/2019/03/15/rohingya-bangladeshs-bhasan-char-will-be-prison (accessed on 22 November 2019).

Ahmed, I. (ed.) 2010. *The Plight of the Stateless Rohingyas*. Dhaka: The University Press Limited.

Ahsan, S.B. 2018. 'The Rohingya Crisis: Why the World Must Act Decisively'. *Asian Affairs*, 49(4): 571–581.

Akhter, S. and K. Kusakabe, 2014. 'Gender-based Violence among Documented Rohingya Refugees in Bangladesh'. *Indian Journal of Gender Studies*, 21(2): 225–246.

Amnesty International. 2018. *Submission for the UN Universal Periodic Review 30th Session of the UPR Working Group, April–May 2018*. NY. UN.

Aparajeyo Bangladesh, Ain o Salish Kendra, ECPAT International, Association for Community Development (ACD). 2017. *Joint NGO Submission to the Third Cycle UPR*. NY: UN.

Arbeiter Samariter-Bund; Centre for Disability Development in Bangladesh; and Aktion Deutschland. 2017. *Rohingya Refugee Crisis in Bangladesh: Age and Disability Inclusion Rapid Assessment Report*. Available at https://www.humanitarianresponse.info/sites/www.humanitarianresponse.info/files/assessments/asbcdd_rohingya_refugee_crisis_-_age_and_disability_inclusion_rapid_assessment_report.pdf (accessed on 12 November 2019).

Beyrer, C. and A. Kamarulzaman. 2017. 'Ethnic Cleansing in Myanmar: The Rohingya Crisis and Human Rights'. *The Lancet*, 30 September, 390(10102): 1570–1573.

Center for Global Non-killing. 2017. *NGO Submission to the Third Cycle UPR*. NY: UN.

Chaney, P. and S. Sahoo. 2020. 'Civil Society and the Contemporary Threat to Religious Freedom in Bangladesh'. *Journal of Civil Society*, 16(3): 191–215.

Chaney, P. 2018. 'Limited Gains, Enduring Violations: Civil Society Perspectives on the Implementation of the United Nations' Convention on the Rights of the Child in Bangladesh'. *Journal of South Asian Development*, 12(3): 47–58.

Child Rights Advocacy Coalition in Bangladesh (CRAC,B). 2017. *NGO Submission to the Third Cycle UPR*. NY: UN.

Chowdhury, M., F. Jahan and R. Rahman. 2017. 'Developing Urban Space: The Changing Role of NGOs in Bangladesh'. *Development in Practice*, 27(2): 82–97.

Christian Solidarity Worldwide. 2017. *NGO Submission to the Third Cycle UPR*. NY: UN.

Cultural Survival and American Indian Law Clinic. 2017. *Observations on the State of Indigenous Human Rights in Bangladesh—NGO Submission to the Third Cycle UPR*. NY: UN.

Friedrich, M. 2018. 'High Rates of Violent Death among Rohingya Refugees'. *Journal of the American Medical Association*, 319(7): 648.

Front Line Defenders. 2017. *NGO Submission to the Third Cycle UPR*. NY: UN.

Government of Bangladesh. 2018. *National report submitted in accordance with paragraph 5 of the annex to Human Rights Council resolution 16/21 –Bangladesh*. NY: UN. Available at A/HRC/WG.6/30/BGD/1 (accessed on 13 January 2021).

Hasan-Ul-Bari, S.M. and T. Ahmed. 2018. 'Ensuring Sexual and Reproductive Health and Rights of Rohingya Women and Girls'. *The Lancet*, 8 December, 392(10163): 2439–2440.

Human Rights Council, Working Group on the Universal Periodic Review. 2013. National report submitted in accordance with paragraph 5 of the annex to Human Rights Council resolution 16/21—Bangladesh, A/HRC/WG.6/16/BGD/1. Geneva: UN, p. 24

_______. 2018. Draft report of the Working Group on the Universal Periodic Review—Bangladesh, A/HRC/WG.6/30/L.10. Geneva: UN.

Human Rights Forum, Bangladesh. 2017. *NGO Submission to the Third Cycle UPR*. NY: UN.

Human Rights Watch. 2017. *NGO Submission to the Third Cycle UPR*. NY: UN.

Institute on Statelessness and Inclusion. 2017. *NGO Submission to the Third Cycle UPR*. NY: UN.

Inter Sector Coordination Group. 2019. *Situation Report Rohingya Refugee Crisis September 2019*. Geneva, ISCG.

International Service for Human Rights. 2017. *NGO Submission to the Third Cycle UPR*. NY: UN.

Kyaw, N.N. 2017. 'Unpacking the Presumed Statelessness of Rohingyas'. *Journal of Immigrant & Refugee Studies*, 15(3): 79–91.

Landry, M. and A. Tupetz. 2018. 'Disability and the Rohingya Displacement Crisis: A Humanitarian Priority'. *Archives of Physical Medicine and Rehabilitation*, 99: 2122–2124.

Leidman, E., A. Humphreys and B. Greene Cramer. 2018. 'Acute Malnutrition and Anemia among Rohingya Children in Kutupalong Camp, Bangladesh'. *JAMA*, 319(14): 1505–1506.

MSNA/ISCG. 2019. *Joint Multi-Sector Needs Assessment–Key Findings: Refugees and Host Communities*, October. Geneva: MSNA/ISCG.

Mahmood, S., E. Wroe, A. Fuller and J. Leaning. 2017. 'The Rohingya People of Myanmar: Health, Human Rights, and Identity'. *Lancet,* 389: 1841–1850.

Milton, A.H., M. Rahman, S. Hussain and C. Jindal. 2017. 'Trapped in Statelessness: Rohingya Refugees in Bangladesh'. *International Journal of Environmental Resources and Public Health*, 14: 942.

Mohajan, H. 2014. 'Child Rights in Bangladesh'. *Journal of Social Welfare and Human Rights*, 2(1): 207–238.

Mukul, S., S. Huq, J. Herbohn, A Nishat, A. Rahman, R. Amin and F. Ahmed. 2019. 'Rohingya Refugees and the Environment'. *Science* (New York, NY), 12 April, 364(6436): 138.

Murphy, D. 2018. 'Stateless: The Rohingya Refugees One Year on'. *British Medical Journal*, 29 August, vol. 362.

Naushin Parnini, S. 2013. 'The Crisis of the Rohingya as a Muslim Minority in Myanmar and Bilateral Relations with Bangladesh.' *Journal of Muslim Minority Affairs*, 33(2): 281–297.

Petcharamesree, S. 2016. 'ASEAN Human Rights Regime and Mainstreaming the Responsibility to Protect: Challenges and Prospects'. *Global Responsibility to Protect*, 8(2–3): 133–157.

Rahman, U. 2010. 'The Rohingya Refugee: A Security Dilemma for Bangladesh'. *Journal of Immigrant & Refugee Studies*, 8(2): 233–239.

Saidul Islam, M. 2011. '"Minority Islam" in Muslim Majority Bangladesh: The Violent Road to a New Brand of Secularism'. *Journal of Muslim Minority Affairs*, 31(1): 43–55.

Solidarity Group for Bangladesh. 2017. *NGO Submission to the Third Cycle UPR*. NY: UN.

_______. 2018. *NGO Submission to the Third Cycle Universal Periodic Review*. Geneva: United Nations.

Suykens, B. 2018. 'A Hundred Per Cent Good Man Cannot Do Politics: Violent Self-Sacrifice, Student Authority, and Party-State Integration in Bangladesh'. *Modern Asian Studies*, 52(3): 883–916.

Uddin, N. 2015. 'State of Stateless People: The Plight of Rohingya Refugees in Bangladesh'. In *The Human Right to Citizenship*, edited by Rhoda

Howard-Hassman and Margaret Walton-Roberts, 62–77. Philadelphia: University of Pennsylvania Press.

United Nations Human Rights Council (UNHRC). 2012. *Bangladesh Second Cycle UPR Report*. NY: UN.

_______. 2018. *Report of the Independent International Fact-Finding Mission on Myanmar*. NY: UN.

_______. 2018. 'UNHCR and UNDP Sign a Memorandum of Understanding (MOU) with Myanmar to Support the Creation of Conditions for the Return of Refugees from Bangladesh'. Joint UNHCR/UNDP Press Release, 6 June. Available at https://www.unhcr.org/news/press/2018/6/5b1787e64/unhcr-undp-sign-memorandum-understanding-mou-myanmar-support-creation-conditions.html (accessed on 13 January 2021).

United Nations Human Rights Council Working Group on the Universal Periodic Review. 2008. Compilation Prepared By the Office of the High Commissioner For Human Rights, In Accordance With Paragraph 15(B) of the Annex to Human Rights Council Resolution 5/1. New York: UN United Nations Human Rights Council.

United Nations (UN) News. 2018. 'Dangers Persist for Nearly a Million Rohingya Refugees in Bangladesh: WHO'. Available at https://news.un.org/en/story/2018/05/1009112 (accessed on 12 November 2019).

United Nations Office for the High Commissioner for Human Rights. 1979. *Convention on the Elimination of All Forms of Discrimination against Women*, New York, OHCHR. Available at https://www.ohchr.org/en/professionalinterest/pages/cedaw.aspx (accessed on 13 January 2021).

United Nations Office for the Coordination of Humanitarian Affairs. 2019. *2019 Joint Response Plan for Rohingya Humanitarian Crisis*. Geneva: OCHA.

Ware, A. and C. Laoutides. 2018. 'The Rohingya "Origin" Narrative'. In *Myanmar's 'Rohingya' Conflict*, edited by Anthony Ware and Costas Laoutides. Oxford Scholarship Online.

Wali, N., C. Wen, L. Rawal, A.S.M. Amanullah and A. Renzaho. 2018. 'Integrating Human Rights Approaches into Public Health Practices and Policies to Address Health Needs amongst Rohingya Refugees in Bangladesh: A Systematic Review and Meta-Ethnographic Analysis'. *Archives of Public Health*, 76(2): 34–41.

White, K. 2017. 'Rohingya in Bangladesh: An Unfolding Public Health Emergency'. *The Lancet*, 28 October, 390(10106): 1947–1947.

World Food Programme. 2018. *Rohingya Refugee Emergency–Food Security Update*, December. Rome: WFP.

Yesmin, S. 2016. 'Policy towards Rohingya Refugees: A Comparative Analysis of Bangladesh, Malaysia and Thailand'. *Journal of the Asiatic Society of Bangladesh* (Hum.), 61(1): 71–100.

4

Cooperation or Conflict? Understanding State–Civil Society Relationship in Postcolonial India

Sarbeswar Sahoo

Following a decade of rule by the Congress-led United Progressive Alliance (UPA) government, which became tainted by a series of corruption scandals towards the end of its second term, the BJP-led National Democratic Alliance (NDA) government came to power in the summer of 2014.[1] The new government under the leadership of Prime Minister Narendra Modi became committed to the principle of inclusive development—*sabka saath, sabka vikas* (together with all, development for all) and promised to bring *achhe din* (good times) for all. The Modi-led NDA government was re-elected in 2019. In the last six years, the government has implemented a model of development that has emphasised not only economic growth but also livelihood security (Baru, 2019). Particularly, it has implemented several developmental programmes for the poor through grassroots civil society groups. While the government has involved civil society groups in its policy implementation process, a section of the civil society still continues to feel neglected and marginalised.

The sphere of civil society, which refers to the non-state sphere of associational life,[2] has become restricted in its scope and functioning. A historical analysis of the state–civil society relationship shows that this is not a new development. We have repeatedly witnessed such repression of the civil society; notably in the 1970s during the regime of Indira Gandhi. Taking a historical perspective, this chapter shows how the relationship between state and civil society in India has undergone significant transformation over the years. Accordingly, the following discussion considers the shifting and often contested relationship between state and civil society over different periods, beginning first with the birth of modern India.

State and Civil Society in the Nehruvian Period

Following independence, India's democratic Constitution gave every citizen the right to freedom of speech, freedom of association and freedom of press, which served as the foundation for the development of a free public sphere. Through various constitutional measures, the modern Indian state also encouraged people to relate to each other without any discrimination. Considering the prevalence of mass poverty, illiteracy and underdevelopment, the Indian state undertook a major role in nation building. Specifically, Nehru considered 'the state as an instrument of *maintenance* in the everyday sphere (improving the quality of people's lives) …' (Fernee, 2012); the dominant belief was that 'a strong state was the only way a mass society, which was largely illiterate and poor, which held strong ethnic and caste loyalties and was hence "incapable" of thinking for the country, could be adequately governed' (Kamat, 2002). The state thus followed a centralised mode of planning and governance. According to Rajni Kothari (2001), the Nehruvian Indian state between 1947 and 1967 was a 'moderate state'—one which despite the powerful tendency towards centralisation and homogenisation, acted as an instrument of social justice and human freedom.[3] Partha Chatterjee (1997) also notes that the period was characterised by a 'developmental state', intervening in the economy, planning and guiding its growth and actively promoting the welfare of its population.

The Gandhian principle of *swaraj* and self-reliance had a major influence on Nehru and the postcolonial state building in India. Affirming self-reliance, Nehru called for building a broad-based civil society by encouraging people's participation in development and nation-building process. As he declared in 1957:

> [I]f there is real democracy in India, we have to involve the maximum number of people in the task of decision-making and implementation .... The modern nations in particular cannot grow unless the responsibility is delegated to the people.... Democracy is not a matter of passing laws, it has to take roots among the people. (Fernee, 2012)

Thus, to encourage people's participation, the state invited Gandhian organisations to play a leading role in national reconstruction and development of village communities and civil societies (Sahoo, 2013b). Through its Five-Year Plans, the state introduced Community Development Programmes[4] and provided large-scale funding to Gandhian organisations that worked in community and rural development. Many religion-based NGOs, youth and women's clubs and secular non-Gandhian NGOs (including branches of international NGOs) also emerged to help the rural poor (Kudva, 2005). The state increased funding for voluntary organisations significantly. Thus, during Nehru's period, Gandhian NGOs played a major role in providing *welfare and relief* and shared a strong and co-operative relationship with the state.

Indira Gandhi's Regime and State–Civil Society Relationship

After the death of Nehru, particularly in the late 1960s, India witnessed a period of political and social instability. The Nehruvian moderate state, which had provided political stability and steered through development planning during the early years of independent India, declined (Kothari, 2001). India witnessed the criminalisation of politics, ineffectiveness in enforcing the rule of law, rising corruption scandals and the decline of democratic institutions. India's economy underwent a deeper crisis as it experienced severe food scarcity and price rises, leading to civil unrest in different parts of the country. At this juncture, the Indian state 'suffered from both a crisis of governability as well as a crisis of legitimacy' (Chandhoke, 2003). Instead of addressing these problems, the government adopted populist politics and used slogans like *garibi hatao* (eradicate poverty) for electoral gain. Furthermore, the emergence of the Naxalite movement challenged the legitimacy of the government. In order to control the political situation, Mrs Indira Gandhi suspended the rule of law and imposed Emergency rule in 1975. During this period, intellectuals, lawyers, journalists, civil society activists and even ordinary citizens were imprisoned arbitrarily and their fundamental rights were heavily curtailed. Moreover, during Emergency, Mrs Gandhi systematically suppressed civil society and undermined the legitimacy of democratic political institutions. Notwithstanding this suppression, several civil society movements at their grassroots level emerged in different parts of the country to resist Mrs Gandhi's authoritarian rule. As D.L. Seth observes:

> The anti-emergency movements gave rise, especially in the period between the mid-1970s and 1980s, to thousands of *new* micro-movements in the country. These movements were led by young men and women, quite a few of whom left their professional careers to join them. They took up issues and constituencies abandoned by political parties and trade unions, and those ill-served by the bureaucracy. The organisational form they evolved for themselves was not of a political party or a pressure group. It was that of a civil-associational group, leading political struggles on issues articulated to them by the people themselves. The key concept they worked with was democratising development through empowerment of the people. (Seth, 2004)

Two of the major civil society movements that emerged during the Emergency are the *Navnirman Andolan* (social transformation/reconstruction movement) in Gujarat and the *Sampoorna Kranti* (total revolution) movement in Bihar (Shah, 2019). Gandhian social activists like Jayaprakash Narayan (known as JP), who led the

Sampoorna Kranti movement, staunchly opposed Mrs Gandhi's rule, as he strongly believed that Mrs Gandhi was primarily responsible for the economic crisis, corruption and centralisation of power. He thus mobilised Gandhian workers, NGOs, students and trade union leaders to become actively involved in the *Sampoorna Kranti* movement to bring political change. More than 300 Gandhian organisations joined the JP movement (Kudva, 2005). JP was also joined by Hindu nationalists (the Rashtriya Swayamsevak Sangh—RSS—and Jan Sangh) and another famous Gandhian called Morarji Desai. Desai played a major role in mobilising the middle classes in his home-state of Gujarat. These rising people's movements at the grassroots level heavily opposed the authoritarian tendencies of the state, which eventually transformed the nature and capacity of the state and civil society in India.

Enactment of the FCRA and Surveillance of the Civil Society

Realising the role that civil society organisations (CSOs) and peoples' movements had been playing in subverting her government, Mrs Gandhi increased control over NGOs and regulated foreign funding. She believed that foreign funding was involved in fuelling anti-state activities in India. In this context, the case of the Asia Foundation, a United States-based agency, came to the fore. The Ministry of Home Affairs (MHA) had granted permission to the Foundation to set up an office in India to provide assistance to various NGOs. It was, however, revealed that the Foundation was funded by the US Central Intelligence Agency (Sen, 1999). Following this shocking disclosure, the government suspended the activities of the Foundation in India. The government also expelled many foreign missionaries and foreign NGO officials, accusing them of subversive activities (Sen, 1999). In consequence, the government enacted the Foreign Contribution Regulation Act

(FCRA) in 1976, aimed at maintaining surveillance of CSOs which received foreign funds.

With the end of the Emergency rule, the Janata Party led by Morarji Desai came to power in 1977. Considering the role CSOs and various peoples' movements had played during the Emergency rule, Desai actively encouraged civil society work and NGO involvement in rural development programmes. The government granted special exceptions and incentives to industries and business to involve CSOs in their activities in rural areas (Ganguly, 2016). It also vastly increased funding for CSOs and provided bureaucratic support. Encouraged by institutional incentives, the country witnessed the proliferation of professional NGOs and voluntary organisations, which provided services to the marginalised communities in the form of health, education, micro-credit and sanitation (Ganguly, 2016). Taking advantage of this, the Hindu nationalists, who were partners of JP during the anti-Emergency movement, also expanded their activities in different parts of India.

However, although the Janata government actively promoted NGOs and other civil society actors, this policy did not last long. Mrs Gandhi returned to power in 1980 and increased control over CSOs. She amended the FCRA in 1984, making it obligatory for all NGOs receiving foreign funds to register themselves with the MHA. This helped the state to monitor NGO activities and empowered it to ban any organisation from receiving foreign contributions, should the state consider the organisation to be 'political' instead of a 'neutral' NGO (Sahoo, 2013a). Mrs Gandhi also appointed the Kudal Commission in 1981 in retaliation against the Gandhian NGOs that had supported the JP movement during the Emergency rule. The Commission made allegation about missing funds against 945 Gandhian NGOs (Sen, 1993; Sahoo, 2013a). Thus, during Mrs Gandhi's regime, civil society became increasingly depoliticised and controlled by the state.

Civil Society as an Effective Service Delivery Mechanism

Following the assassination of Mrs Gandhi on 31 October 1984, her elder son Rajiv Gandhi came to power with a massive mandate in 1984 General Election. Rajiv Gandhi understood the problems associated with the state-led, top-down approach to development and, hence, advocated for a bottom-up approach. He actively promoted NGOs and other CSOs' delivery of services and role as democratic watchdogs. The Planning Commission also identified NGOs as effective service delivery mechanisms and active partners in development. The Rajiv Gandhi government increased funds available to NGOs and CSOs that worked for social development. Thus,

> the 1980s and 1990s saw rapid development in the voluntary sector because of a supportive government and growing funding by both national and international donors.[5] In addition, there was a changing conception of the development paradigm that centred on increasing people's participation in the implementation of programs and management of resources. (Ganguly, 2016)

Although Rajiv Gandhi was killed during an election campaign in 1991, successive governments continued to recognise the role of CSOs as partners in development.

Economic Liberalisation and the Further Depoliticisation of Civil Society

With the liberalisation of Indian economy in the early 1990s, the World Bank and the International Monetary Fund (IMF) became interested in the poverty alleviation project. They blamed the state and rigid bureaucracies of the Third World for being responsible for the persistence of poverty (Sahoo, 2013b). The World Bank President, Robert McNamara, had declared in the late 1960s that 'the Third World States were not capable and efficient in carrying out development works for the poor' (Shah, 2019). Considering the failure of the Third World states to tackle the problem of poverty, the World Bank and the IMF invited CSOs to play a major role in this regard. However, by promoting CSOs, the World Bank, the IMF and other aid agencies also 'depoliticised' civil society and processes of local development (Kamat, 2002). Their major objective was the expansion of international capital into every nook and corner of the world and removal of any resistance to it. In this regard, India, by following structural adjustment conditionalities in 1991, agreed to promote the NGO sector and limit the forms of agitational (*andolanatmak*) civil society as a part of the global agenda of so-called 'good governance' (Sahoo, 2013b). As a consequence of this global agenda, foreign funding to NGOs increased significantly after the 1990s, resulting in what some scholars have termed as 'NGO-ification' of civil society and grassroots politics (Kudva, 2005). Easy availability and increased funding to the NGO sector also turned development into a business and profit-making activity. As Goswami and Tandan (2013) have observed:

> Many organizations have emerged abruptly without being aware of the local context and its needs. Many more, instead of pursuing social commitments, pursue business and commercial motivations. Another prevailing trend is for political leaders to form CSOs. Many CSOs are set up by ex-bureaucrats, ex-corporate employees, and industrialists who have no vision for development or welfare and who regard the sector from a business or profit-making perspective. Some unemployed youth view CSOs and NGOs as self-employment ventures and money-making machines.

Data show that over 3.2 million so-called 'non-profit' and voluntary organisations are registered in India today,[6] making it 'the unofficial NGO capital of the world' (Parekh, 2001). A recent study published in *LiveMint* newspaper, however, pointed out that 'the NGO sector has emerged as a competitive employer and offers meaningful and attractive opportunities for employees' (Mathur, 2017). It noted:

> Many of the NGOs are being run as rigorously as corporate organizations, incorporating practices such as compensation benchmarking, performance management and training-need analysis for all employees. Training programmes focusing on leadership development, behavioural training, managerial skill development and opportunities for vocational learning are offered to employees. Benefits like financial help in times of a family crisis, free medical facilities in affiliated hospitals and aid to school-going children of employees are also made available. (Mathur, 2017)

Increased development aid and favourable donor policies were largely responsible for the corporatisation of the NGO sector. Some NGO entrepreneurs took the easy availability of international funding as an opportunity to *professionalise* service delivery and development activities for the poor. With this, many NGOs, which formed a vital part of civil society, shifted away from their initial role of being the 'watchdog of society' to an apolitical, professionalised service delivery role. Several of the NGOs were also being co-opted by the state. This, however, does not mean all NGOs followed this route. While it is true that the major trend has been the de-politicisation of NGOs and civil society, there are some NGOs and grassroots civil society groups that have been constantly engaged in political mobilisation to make the state more accountable and development more inclusive (Katyaini, Van Wessel and Sahoo, 2021). Very often, such mobilisation takes the form of a social movement and seeks to force the government to change its policies and systems of governance. Key examples include the anti-corruption movement in Delhi, the anti-POSCO movement in Odisha and the Singur movement against land acquisition in West Bengal. Besides this, the state also *collaborates* (not, co-opt) with CSOs as active partners in development (Van Wessel, Naz and Sahoo, 2020). A major boost came to state–civil society partnership when the Congress-led UPA government came to power in 2004;

it actively collaborated with civil society groups not just to implement projects but also to formulate pro-poor development policies through its Common Minimum Programme.

Civil Society under the Congress-led UPA Regime

Two paradoxical developments occurred during the decade long Congress-led UPA government that had significant implications for state–civil society relations in India.

One the one hand, the government actively promoted civil society groups as partners of development. Acting in this direction, in 2007, the Manmohan Singh government passed the first ever National Policy on Voluntary Sector in India, which proposed to create 'an enabling environment for voluntary organizations by regular consultations with various national ministries' (Goswami and Tandan, 2013). The government not only consulted CSOs on various occasions but also actively involved them in its pro-poor policy-making process. It created a special body called the National Advisory Council (NAC) consisting of ex-bureaucrats, academics and civil society activists to advise the government on formulating and implementing its pro-poor agenda codified through the Common Minimum Programme. The NAC played a major role in facilitating the relationship between the government and the civil society. It specifically followed a rights-based approach and played an instrumental role in drafting several key pro-poor laws like the Right to Information Act (2005), the National Rural Employment Guarantee Act (2005), the Forest Rights Act (2006), the Right to Education Act (2009) and the National Food Security Act (2013). According to Khera (2020), the introduction of such laws to some extent shifted the 'model of welfare provision from one of state benevolence to a rights-based system'. Moreover, these laws not only advanced a 'rights-based approach to development' but it also strengthened 'the roots of democracy' at the local level by providing 'increased scope for citizen-led transparency and accountability in governance systems' (Goswami and Tandan, 2013).

On the other hand, the government was strongly committed to the implementation of neoliberal economic policies in India.[7] In order to achieve and maintain high economic growth, the government invited multinational companies and facilitated their entry into resource rich regions. This growth model required large-scale acquisition of land, which was not easy because of the existence of the colonial era Land Acquisition Act of 1894. The UPA government, therefore, amended the old Act and introduced the new Land Acquisition and Rehabilitation and Resettlement Act (LARRA) of 2013[8] to facilitate land acquisition for commercial and development projects. The new Act was a significant improvement over the old one and struck 'a balance between the industrialization and infrastructural drive of the government and legitimate compensation for the displaced people' (Mukerji, 2017).

However, acquisition of land for infrastructural development, real estate and township projects, special economic zones and mining projects (for example, by POSCO and Vedanta) created massive displacements and dislocations. This eventually resulted in large-scale civil society protests against the exclusivist and exploitative policies of neoliberalism. Several NGOs and grassroots organisations criticised the government for its anti-people policies and mobilised the marginalised against the state. They organised non-violent demonstrations, strikes and protest marches in front of government offices. Knowing that the NGOs and other civil society groups were playing a major role in leading such anti-state and 'anti-development' protest movements, the government tightened its rules, and regulated the roles of and resources available to CSOs. Those NGOs that received foreign funding were controlled by the FCRA rules (Van Wessel, Naz and Sahoo, 2020). Yet, to increase its control over civil society, the government enacted the new FCRA in 2010. Its objective was to largely restrict NGOs' role to depoliticised service delivery activities. As Chacko (2018) rightly notes, '[R]ather than democratizing policy making … the UPA's tendency was towards authoritarian statist forms of depoliticized and technocratic forms of governance'.

The NDA Regime, Neoliberalism and Civil Society

Following the Congress-led UPA government, the BJP-led NDA government has aggressively followed the neoliberal policies and promoted the interests of domestic and international capital. As observers of Indian politics know, the Modi government has actively promoted pro-business policies. The 'Make in India' campaign aptly reflects the government's growth model, which aims to promote foreign direct investment, boost innovation and develop the manufacturing sector.[9] Through this campaign, the government seeks to present a 'new mindset' where it will no longer be seen as a regulator (as it has been traditionally viewed) but regarded as a facilitator. The fundamental objective of this shift in emphasis 'was to give additional push to privatization and global engagement so as to create an investor-friendly environment and turn the economy into global manufacturing powerhouse' (Mukerji, 2017). Doing so required further amendments to the LARRA of 2013. Soon after coming to power, the BJP government promulgated a land ordinance on 31 December 2014 where it identified five categories of land use such as: defence, rural infrastructure, housing for poor, industrial corridor and PPP projects. Crucially, these would be exempted from the various modes of conditionality under the LARRA, 2013 (Mukerji, 2017). The opposition political parties and CSOs resisted to some of the changes proposed by the government. Nevertheless, the government made some amendments and passed the Bill (named Right to Fair Compensation, Transparency in Land Acquisition, Rehabilitation and Resettlement, 2015).

This shows that active promotion of neoliberal interests have depoliticised and restricted the role of civil society. In particular, it should be noted that regardless of whichever political party—the Congress or the BJP—is in power, contemporary Indian history tells us that the state has actively promoted the interests of private capital in the name of development and economic growth (Sahoo, 2017). Neoliberal policies (and crony capitalism) have led to heavy commodification of land, consequently giving rise to land grabbing in rural India. 'While the social and political structures [have become] subordinated to market laws and logic, the role of the state [have become] limited to that of a "night-watchman", or enforcer of market rules' (Sahoo, 2017). The state has been using its power (including its coercive apparatus) to facilitate and acquire land for market forces. For example, the Gujarat government has, 'helped to acquire 15,946 acres of land for the Adani Group, 1,100 acres for Tata Motors, 460 acres for Ford India, and 700 acres for Maruti Suzuki for industrial and SEZ purposes at extremely low prices' (Sahoo, 2017). Similarly, 'the state government of Odisha promised to acquire 4,000 acres of land for POSCO, a South Korean steel company, to set up a steel plant and build port infrastructure' (Sahoo, 2017).[10]

Today, large-scale acquisition of land for mining, industry, infrastructure and special economic zones have adversely affected millions of poor Indians and displaced them from their land, undermining their livelihoods and rights. As a reaction to such exclusivist and exploitative neoliberal policies, several NGOs and peoples' movements have emerged in different parts of the country to stand up for the socioeconomic and citizenship rights of the marginalised. The BJP government, which aims to bring rapid industrialisation and economic development, finds such oppositional/politicised civil society groups and people's movements an obstacle to the process of development and nation building. In a leaked 2014 report, India's Intelligence Bureau accused NGOs of 'reducing India's GDP by a staggering 2 to 3 per cent per annum, by campaigning against projects that the Indian government argued to be integral to economic growth' (Doane, 2016). The report also accused 'foreign funded' NGOs such as Greenpeace, Amnesty, Cordaid and ActionAid of 'serving as tools for foreign policy interests of western governments' by sponsoring campaigns to protect the environment or support human rights (Doane, 2016).

While the state is open to collaboration with apolitical and welfare-oriented civil society groups or groups that support its political agenda, in general, it considers politicised CSOs a threat to its legitimacy and sovereignty. As Behar (2019) rightly observes, the 'invited space' of collaboration for civil society groups in policy-making and governance has been shrinking over the years. The

> underlying assumption behind [the] push for the invited space is that participation can significantly enhance the state's performance by making it both more responsive and more accountable. Increased dialogue and consultation between the state and citizens could help ensure that local needs and demands are heard and that decision makers have better feedback on effectiveness of their decision. (Aiyar, 2010)

The question is, what kinds of forces dominate the sphere of civil society and what kinds of interests are they representing? Considering this, the present government is replacing the *old* civil society groups with a *new* set of actors like the India Foundation and the Vivekananda International Foundation that are close to the government's ideology and support its development agenda (Behar, 2019).

Amendments to FCRA and Autonomy of the Civil Society

In order to monitor the activities of CSOs, the Congress-led UPA government had enacted the FCRA 2010 by replacing the FCRA of 1976. The Congress government had claimed that the new Act was introduced to make it easier for the private sector and CSOs to receive foreign funds. However, the Act made it compulsory for NGOs to register with the MHA if they intended to receive foreign funding. This empowered the MHA 'to suspend, cancel or freeze the FCRA account of an organisation if it is determined that the organisation violated any provision of the FCRA' (CIVICUS, 2017). After the BJP government came to power, it made the FCRA rules stricter. In 2015, the government made further amendments to the FCRA rules which:

> ... increased the reporting requirements for CSOs and made it compulsory for all registration applications to be made online. Under the amended rules, all organisations that receive funding from foreign sources must also publish annual audit statements of the funds, stating what the funds were used for, on their official website or a website specified by the central government. The statements must include details of the donors, amounts received and dates donations were received. In addition, Indian banks are compelled to report any funds received from foreign sources within 48 hours. (CIVICUS, 2017)

These amendments and provisions made it easy for the government to monitor the activities of CSOs. As Paul Chaney (2019), based on a study of submissions to the United Nations' third cycle of Universal Period Review (UPR) 2012–2017, has shown, Indian CSOs have continually revealed 'concerns over the weakening of rule of law institutions and restrictions on civil society', especially CSOs that work on human rights and religious freedom issues.[11] In 2016, the MHA cancelled the registration of Lawyers Collective, an NGO that works on human rights issues. The Lawyers Collective and its founders were accused of mis-utilising funds received under the FCRA. Similarly, in April 2015, the MHA ordered to freeze the bank accounts of Greenpeace India and accused the organisation 'of engaging in activities that were against India's economic interests, threatening national security and inciting protests' (CIVICUS, 2017).

Reports show that between 5 May and 9 June 2015, the MHA cancelled the registration of 4,470 CSOs for violating the FCRA (CIVICUS, 2017). Furthermore, in 2016, the government cancelled licences of around 20,000 of 33,000 NGOs after they were found to be violating various provisions of the FCRA (*The Times of India*, 2016). Here it should be noted that the FCRA is not the only instrument used by the government to control and monitor civil society; it has also used income tax authorities to question several civil society groups (Behar, 2019). Furthermore, to control international funding to Indian NGOs, the government has frozen bank accounts/ transactions of several NGOs and put 17 large funding agencies on the prohibited list, including entities like the Ford Foundation, Open Society, Compassion International,[12] IDRC, HIVOS and Greenpeace International (Behar, 2019).[13] As a result, foreign funding to NGOs was reduced by about 60 per cent from 2014 to 2017 (Arora, 2020). This shows how the government has 'weakened the grassroots base of progressive civil society by starving it of resources' (Behar, 2019).

Concluding Remarks

The foregoing discussion shows the antecedents to the contemporary restriction on the civic space in India. In the latest CIVICUS Global Report (2019), India has been downgraded in the civic space rating from 'obstructed' to 'repressed' due to 'increased restriction of space for dissent'. As the chapter demonstrated, such restrictions on the scope and functioning of civil society is nothing new. Though the state and civil society enjoyed a very cooperative and constructive relationship during the Nehruvian period, it was during the regime of Mrs Indira Gandhi that civil society experienced restrictions and repression through the enactment of the FCRA. Various successive governments have emulated this and also utilised the FCRA as an instrument to coerce and constrain the civil society. The space for autonomous CSOs—especially those working on human rights, safeguarding the environment and climate change and indigenous workers' rights and minority rights—is shrinking.

Whilst today, the liberal traditions (that of De Tocqueville) and neoliberal institutions (such as the World Bank and the IMF) view CSOs as a universal force for democracy, good governance and equal citizenship, all kinds of civil society forces do not necessarily contribute positively towards democratic development. The domain of civil society is inherently pluralistic, which may also contain some 'uncivil' forces. Thus, there is an urgent need for greater discernment.

Notes

1. This chapter draws heavily from my previous work on civil society (see Sahoo, 2013a). I would like to thank Vedi R. Hadiz and Paul Chaney for their comments on an earlier draft of this chapter.
2. It should be noted here that civil society is not a monolithic concept; it is inherently pluralistic and heterogeneous and includes all kinds associations (Sahoo, 2019). Specifically, it is a space

   > where voluntary and primordial, civil and uncivil, hegemonic and counter-hegemonic, political and apolitical, and legal and non-legal groups exercise their interests and carry forward their struggles. It is a sphere where organizations are involved in advancing the interests of people rather than for political power, ranging from those of their members to the more general interest of wider groups in society. (Sahoo, 2014)

   See also Chaney and Sahoo (2020) for a review on the varied conceptions of civil society.
3. In contrast to Kothari, Khera (2020), however, argues that for much of the 70 years of independence, the Indian state has followed a *mai-baap sarkar* (lord and master) attitude. For her, the state is 'viewed as the lord and master of the people' and citizens as 'supplicants at the feet of the state'. Furthermore, 'in this style of governing, any redistribution of resources is based on the whims of the lord and master and is viewed as an act of state benevolence'.
4. The unintended consequence of government's community development and agriculture extension programmes was that, as Shah (2019) argues, the dominant castes increased their grip over the local power structure.

5. See Van Wessel, Naz and Sahoo (2020) for a discussion on complementarity and collaboration between Indian and international CSOs.
6. https://www.livemint.com/Politics/mYL4EzcxBytudTjvTIOIJN/New-guidelines-for-regulating-NGOs-formulated-Centre-tells.html (accessed on 27 May 2020).
7. Neoliberalisation refers

   > to processes of regulatory restructuring of the state to promote international competitiveness and market principles.... Rather than involving the withdrawal of the state or diminishing its influence processes of neoliberalization require active state intervention to, for instance, create sustain markets and facilitate the transnationalization of domestic capital. (Chacko, 2018)

8. The new Act not only required the consent of the affected families, but also made provisions of social assessment and increased compensation rate for acquired land (Mukerji, 2017).
9. https://www.makeinindia.com/article/-/v/make-in-india-reason-vision-for-the-initiative (accessed on 27 May 2020). In order to increase productivity and reduce imports, Prime Minister Modi has recently called for 'Made in India, Made for the World' campaign; https://www.ndtv.com/video/news/news/made-in-india-made-for-world-pm-modi-s-call-to-reduce-imports-550492?video-featured (accessed on 2 June 2020).
10. It should be noted here that the Odisha government has finally suspended the POSCO project, as it failed to acquire land for the company due to people's resistance.
11. Submissions to UPR help us understand the priorities CSOs attach to different rights violations or what Chaney calls 'pathologies'. According to Chaney (2019), some of the major pathologies or rights violations are: violence; authorities' failure to uphold religious freedom; discrimination, (in)equality and oppression; human rights incompatibility of current laws; restrictions on civil society; government failure to respond to earlier UPR recommendations; forced conversion issues and incitement.
12. Compassion International 'was accused of facilitating religious conversion and told to shut down' (see Arora, 2020).

13. After lobbying and negotiations with the government, some of these funding agencies have been given permission to operate in India, but a large number of them continue to be on the blacklist (Behar, 2019).

References

Aiyar, Y. 2010. 'Invited Spaces, Invited Participation: Effects of Greater Participation on Accountability in Service Delivery'. *India Review,* 9(2): 204–229.

Arora, R. 2020. 'Rule-Bound Governance Matters'. *D+C Development and Cooperation,* 25 March. Available at https://www.dandc.eu/en/article/civil-society-space-shrinking-india-oda-agencies-should-consider-their-stance (accessed on 23 May 2020).

Baru, S. 2019. 'Poor Put Faith in Powerful Modi'. *Civil Society,* 30 May. Available at https://www.civilsocietyonline.com/cover-story/poor-put-faith-in-powerful-modi/ (accessed on 14 January 2021).

Behar, A. 2019. 'The Shrinking Civil Society Space: Re-engineering the Architecture of Democratic India'. In *Re-forming India: The Nation Today,* edited by N.G. Jayal, 404–419. New Delhi: Penguin-Viking.

Chacko, P. 2018. 'The Right Turn in India: Authoritarianism, Populism and Neoliberalization'. *Journal of Contemporary Asia,* 48(4): 541–565.

Chandhoke, N. 2003. 'Governance and the Pluralisation of the State: Implications for Democratic Citizenship'. *Economic and Political Weekly,* 38(28): 2957–2968.

Chaney, P. 2019. 'India at the Crossroads? Civil Society, Human Rights and Religious Freedom: Critical Analysis of CSOs' Third Cycle Universal Periodic Review Discourse 2012–2017'. *The International Journal of Human Rights,* 24(5): 531–562.

Chaney, P. and S. Sahoo. 2020. 'Civil Society and the Contemporary Threat to Religious Freedom in Bangladesh'. *Journal of Civil Society,* 16(3): 191–215.

Chatterjee, P. 1997. 'Introduction: A Political History of Independent India'. In *State and Politics in India,* edited by P. Chatterjee, 1–39. New Delhi: Oxford University Press.

CIVICUS. 2017. *India: Democracy Threatened by Growing Attacks on Civil Society.* CIVICUS Publications, November.

______. 2019. *People Power Under Attack: A Report Based on Data from the CIVICUS Monitor.* CIVICUS Publications. Available at https://civicus.contentfiles.net/media/assets/file/GlobalReport2019.pdf (accessed on 23 May 2020).

Doane, D. 2016. 'The Indian Government Has Shut the Door on NGOs'. *The Guardian,* 7 September. Available at https://www.theguardian.com/global-development-professionals-network/2016/sep/07/the-indian-government-has-shut-the-door-on-ngos (accessed on 25 February 2020).

Fernee, T. 2012. 'The Common Theoretical Terrain of the Gandhi and Nehru Periods: The Ethic of Reconciliation over Revenge in Nation-making'. *Studies in History,* 28(1): 117–128.

Ganguly, S. 2016. *Deliberating Environment Policy in India: Participation and the Role of Advocacy.* London: Routledge.

Goswami, D. and R. Tandan. 2013. 'Civil Society in Changing India: Emerging Roles, Relationships and Strategies'. *Development in Practice,* 23(5–6): 653–664.

Kamat, S. 2002. *Development Hegemony: NGOs and the State in India.* New Delhi: Oxford University Press.

Katyaini, S., M. Van Wessel and S. Sahoo. 2021. 'Representation by Development Organisations: Evidence from India and Implications for Inclusive Development'. *Journal of Environment and Development,* 30(1): 98–123.

Khera, R. 2020. 'India's Welfare State: A Halting Shift from Benevolence to Rights'. *Current History,* 119(816): 134–140.

Kothari, R. 2001. 'The Crisis of the Moderate State and the Decline of Democracy'. In *Democracy in India,* edited by N.G. Jayal, 101–127. New Delhi: Oxford University Press.

Kudva, N. 2005. 'Strong States, Strong NGOs'. In *Social Movement in India,* edited by R. Ray and M.F. Katzenstein, 233–265. Lanham: Rowman and Littlefield.

Mathur, N. 2017. 'NGOs Fast Emerging as Great Employers'. *LiveMint,* 6 October. Available at https://www.livemint.com/Industry/OrBAPmuDQs8CgCRcgLy3vK/NGOs-fast-emerging-as-great-employers.html (accessed on 25 May 2020).

Mukerji, S. 2017. 'Land Acquisition in Contemporary India: The Growth Agenda, Legislation and Resistance'. *Indian Journal of Public Administration,* 63(1): 85–103.

Parekh, B. 2001. 'A Political Audit of Independent India'. *The Round Table,* 362: 701–709.

Sahoo, S. 2013a. *Civil Society and Democratization in India: Institutions, Ideologies and Interests.* London: Routledge.

______. 2013b. 'Doing Development or Creating Dependency? NGOs and Civil Society in India'. *South Asia: Journal of South Asian Studies,* 36(2): 258–272.

______. 2014. 'Civil Society and Democratization: A Counter-case from India'. *Democratization,* 21(3): 480–500.

______. 2017. Market Liberalism, Marginalized Citizens and Countermovements in India'. *Asian Studies Review,* 41(1): 1–19.

______. 2019. 'The Multiple Faces of Civil Society in India'. In *Civil Society in Global South,* edited by Palash Kamruzzaman, 104–119. London: Routledge.

Sen, S. 1993. 'Defining the Nonprofit Sector: India.' In *Working Papers of the Johns Hopkins Comparative Nonprofit Sector Project,* edited by L.M. Salamon and H.K. Anheier, 1–33. Baltimore: The Johns Hopkins Institute for Policy Studies.

______. 1999. 'Some Aspects of State-NGO Relationship in India in the Post-Independence Era'. *Development and Change,* 30(2): 327–355.

Shah, G. 2019. *Democracy, Civil Society and Governance.* New Delhi: Sage Publications.

Seth, D.L. 2004. 'Globalization and New Politics of Micro-Movements'. *Economic and Political Weekly,* 39(1): 45–58.

The Times of India. 2016. 'FCRA Licenses of 20,000 NGOs Cancelled'. *The Times of India,* 27 December. Available at https://timesofindia.indiatimes.com/india/fcra-licences-of-20000-ngos-cancelled/articleshow/56203438.cms (accessed on 25 February 2020).

Van Wessel, M., F. Naz and S. Sahoo. 2020. 'Complementarities in CSO Collaborations: How Working with Diversity Produces Advantages'. *VOLUNTAS: International Journal of Voluntary and Non-Profit Organizations,* 5 May.

5

The State, NGOs and Civil Society in Bangladesh: Exploring Diverse Trajectories of Interaction

M. Saiful Islam and Md Fouad Hossain Sarker

This chapter examines the diverse trajectories of interaction between the state and the civil society organisations in Bangladesh. Drawing upon political transformation of the state of Bangladesh since independence in 1971, we explore how political changes have determined the state–civil society interaction at different historical junctures; such as, collaboration in the 1970s, followed by suppression, adopting a 'carrot and stick' policy during the military regime in the 1980s and, finally, confrontation and corporatisation in the 1990s and beyond. It is argued that whilst NGOs and civil society organisations are considered to be independent of the state, market and politics, they are being co-opted, suppressed and intimately drawn into politics and business in Bangladesh.

The initial backdrop to the shifting position of civil society in relation to the state began in the wake of the nine-month long war of liberation in 1971. At this point, Bangladesh inherited an economy of complete devastation. Almost everything was shattered and the newly formed government, under the leadership of Bangabandhu Sheikh Mujibur Rahman, had to start with a state of crisis. With declining government revenue, it was almost impossible to feed millions of people, take care of the orphans, widows and refugees returning from India, build devastated infrastructure and ensure minimum public services. Against this backdrop, government invited international assistance which prompted an immediate and massive response from international development and humanitarian organisations. Consequently, a large number of NGOs emerged to help the state and international organisations in delivering services, especially relief and rehabilitation activities. Since then, NGOs have not only gained prominence in the development sector, but their successful service interventions have benefitted millions of people (Abed and Chowdhury, 1997; Lovell, 1992; Blair, 2005; Islam, 2004).

Although it is difficult to estimate exactly how many NGOs are currently operating in Bangladesh, Jamil (1998) reports that there are 816 foreign and local NGOs; whereas, Association of Development Agencies in Bangladesh (ADAB) records a total of 886. In contrast, Ahmed (2003) estimates a total of 1,132 local and foreign NGOs. Whatever the true number be, there is no denying the fact that NGO activities have burgeoned in Bangladesh since independence in 1971 (Islam, 2015).

Over the last 50 years, with the political transition of Bangladesh, interaction between the state and civil society organisations (including NGOs) has gone through several phases of transformation. Accordingly, this chapter seeks to understand the changing relationship between the state and civil society organisations in Bangladesh, a narrative that, as noted, passes through different stages of cooperation, suppression, confrontation and corporatisation (Hashemi, 1993; White, 1999; Tasnim, 2017). We argue that although NGOs and civil society organisations are rhetorically understood to be apolitical, they frequently encounter confrontation with the state and politics while pursuing claim-making and seeking to uphold the rights of the oppressed. Interactions with the state are, thereby, shaped by their mutual interests, which is predominantly dependent upon larger political machinations and ideological contexts. The transition of the NGOs in Bangladesh from relief and rehabilitation service providers in the 1970s to a more corporatised set of organisations in the 1990s does not only reflect the changing philosophies of these NGOs, but also the changing relationship between the state, civil society and international aid in Bangladesh. Such corporatisation of the NGO sector is not merely a coincidence; rather, it is a reflection of the policies of the World Bank, IMF and other international donor institutions, which seek to roll back the state and promote NGOs in the belief that they are flexible, less corrupt and engender citizen trust. Furthermore, since the 1980s, a free-market ideology and structural adjustment programmes have been superimposed on Bangladesh by the IMF and other international donor organisations. The effect has been a reinforcement of neoliberalism that has led to a mushrooming of the NGOs. Our present discussion of the Bangladeshi case has wider international resonance for, in classical theoretical terms, the corporatisation of NGOs and the drive for profit and self-sufficiency challenges the very nature of the NGOs as non-profit development organisations.

In terms of the ensuing structure of this chapter, in order to better understand the trajectories of interaction between the state and the civil society organisations, it is important that we first conceptualise civil society with reference to its origins, definition and function. The discussion then moves on to analyse the nature, extent and emergence of civil society organisations in Bangladesh with specific reference to their relationship with the state. It then describes the first phase of interaction with the state in the 1970s which was cooperative and collaborative. It is followed by a discussion about how civil society organisations were subsequently suppressed by the military regime of the 1980s. A return to democracy in the 1990s saw NGOs being corporatised and aligned with political parties, leading to conflict and contestation. Following this, we reflect on how transformation in the political power of the state at different periods has brought changes in the nature and implications of interaction between the state and civil society organisations in Bangladesh.

Civil Society: A Conceptual Discussion

Although civil society has long been a buzzword in the development literature (Hyden, 1997; Kumar, 1993), it is a contested concept. The definitional trajectory of civil society can be divided into two broad time periods: the classical explanations by Hobbes and Locke, followed by the modern usage by Thomas Paine, Georg Hegel, Alexis De Tocqueville and others. From a classical point of view, civil society has been defined as groups that are formed for collective purposes and primarily located outside of the state and marketplace (Klein and Lee, 2019). However, the definition of civil society continues to change with the transformation of the modern state. It has been variously defined at different historical junctures by different scholars, including Hobbes, Locke and Rousseau. According to Hobbes (Hyden, 1997), the state of nature is an eternal war where people suffer from fear, insecurity and uncertainty. As a result, Hobbes (Tester, 2014) proposed the need for a social contract that would ensure peaceful mutual coexistence between the civil and political spheres. Such a contract entails responsibility and constraints, not least to teach people the value of maintaining sovereignty and protecting it (Arato, 1989). Thus, according to such views, civil society is an artificial construct, which stands as the antithesis of the precarious state of nature. According to Hobbes and Locke, civil and political society are mutually supportive and do not necessarily stand in opposition. On the other hand, Rousseau (Grimsley, 1973) argues that there is a hidden prince or noble savage in each human being which needs to be nurtured. His famous statement '... man is born free, but everywhere he is in chains' reflects how human beings are constrained by the societal norms from which they need to be liberated (Grimsley, 1973; DeWiel, 1997). Thus, Rousseau identified civil society as a space independent of the state of nature (Tester, 2014). Following Hobbes, Locke argued that state of nature is not necessarily a continuous war; rather, it is a state of condition where people enjoy a peaceful environment and can protect their property. However, nobody can enjoy such a peaceful environment in a secured and guaranteed manner due to lack of centralised authority and constraints (Chandhoke, 1995; Tester, 2014). Thus, according to this view, the emergence of the state is nothing but the creation of necessary constraints to maintain law and order.

More modern conceptualisations of civil society come from Hegel, Marx, Gramsci, Tocqueville and others. From a Hegelian point of view (Whitehead, 1997; Neocleous, 1995), civil society is different from political society, and guided mostly by the socioeconomic and material aspirations of the self-seeking human being. Civil society thus stands in between the patriarchal family and the universal state. Karl Marx, although heavily influenced by Hegel, sees civil society as 'the true source and theatre of all history' (Comaroff and Comaroff, 1999). Whilst viewed from a Marxian point of view, civil society is an arena of struggle between privileged and underprivileged classes. However, in crucial distinction to some earlier scholars, Marx identifies civil society as nothing but an extension of the state, which serves the interest of the bourgeoisie class and, thus, it is a sphere where two self-interested men meet each other (Chandhoke, 1995). Moving away from a Marxian economic perspective, Antonio Gramsci (Anderson, 1976) offers further insight by seeing civil society as a sphere of state hegemony, which may not necessarily belong to the economic 'base', but to the ideological and cultural 'superstructure' of the society. In the Gramscian perspective, the state is a political society, which is coercive and dominating by virtue of its control over police, prison and military forces; civil society, on the other hand, is the arena of cultural hegemony which is constituted of educational and cultural systems, mass media and activities of the 'organic intellectuals' (DeWiel, 1997; Kumar, 1993).

Finally, a more liberal conceptualisation of civil society comes from Alexis de Tocqueville and Neo-Tocquevillians such as Putnam (1993) and Fukuyama (1995) who focus on the realm of associations and social capital. Tocqueville argues that (Kumar, 1993) civil society is essentially a 'political society' constituted by 'the art of association', which includes such political associations as local self-government, parties and public opinion; whereas, civil associations are composed of churches, literary and scientific societies, media, professional bodies and organisations. States can be hegemonic and repressive to the people through totalitarian rule; therefore, civil society plays a crucial role as a form of protection against state domination and a counter balance to help keep the state accountable and effective (Adamson, 1980).

Having taken into consideration these differing conceptual trajectories of civil society, Sahoo (2013) has identified three different faces of civil society in the context of India: liberal pluralist, neo-Marxist and communitarian. Liberal pluralist civil society refers to the autonomous and intermediary agencies between the citizens and the state, which often share a cooperative relationship with the state and may not necessarily challenge the hegemony of the state and the existing power structure. Neo-Marxist civil society organisations act as a 'counter-hegemonic' force to redress state coercion, unequal power relations and structural problems. Under this form of civil society, organisations emphasise claim-making and the rights of the oppressed. As a consequence, they often encounter confrontation with the state. Lastly, under communitarian civil society, its organisations focus on strengthening moral values and bonds in order to reinforce shared collective conscience to build a good society. Communitarian politics are beneficial when they uphold community interest over individualism. Yet, they can also be bad when they fuel communal antagonism, intolerance and demonise 'others' as enemies (Sahoo, 2014).

Despite these conceptual variants of the civil society, here we understand civil society as a private, non-state institution or political space between the state and family which works independently of the state for the protection and advancement of civil rights, freedom and public interest (Gellner, 1994; Keane, 1988; Hamilton, 1994). Accordingly, civil society is expected to play a crucial role in broadening citizens' political involvement, working to ensure government responsibility, promoting democratic citizenship and supporting development initiatives (Quadir, 2015). Our view is also cognisant of the fact that civil society organisations may not necessarily contribute to 'civility' or 'good society' (see Kwon, 2004; Sahoo, 2013). For this study, we find Sahoo's conceptualisation of civil society organisations (2013) particularly useful in understanding state–civil society interactions in Bangladesh. As the following discussion reveals, we argue that there are multiple civil society organisations in Bangladesh and their interaction and relationship with the state has been shaped by prevailing politico-ideological contexts, which have resulted in various stages of cooperation, suppression and confrontation.

Civil Society in Bangladesh

Bangladesh has a tradition of both 'old' and 'new' forms of civil societies (Lewis, 2004). The old civil societies could be traced back to non-institutional forms of cooperation, church and missionary activities, the Muslim zakat system and other forms of religious, voluntary and philanthropic activities. Palli Mangal Samiti[1] in the 1930s could be recognised as the antecedent of contemporary development approaches to promote well-being of the poor. Civil society also played an important role at different crisis periods in the country, for example, during the language movement in 1952, mass movement in 1969 and in the liberation war in 1971.[2] However, the most recent form of civil society could be identified as originating in 1971 against the backdrop of a national emergency after the liberation war to reconstruct war-damaged Bangladesh. The economy was stalled and the infrastructure was devastated as millions of people were affected by the nine-month long war. The government had to seek support from the international development organisations to rebuild the infrastructure and economy. Mostly supported and funded by international donor organisations, NGOs and civil society organisations initiated a new phase of development intervention in Bangladesh. Since then, civil society has experienced a diversified interaction with the state and other international donor organisations. Civil society organisations, which originated with the goal of relief and rehabilitation programmes, became highly politicised in the 1990s by being directly aligned with different political parties.

Since the 1990s, civil society in Bangladesh has strengthened its role by reinforcing its presence via social and electronic media, shaping newspaper opinion and using popular blog channels to demand better governance, a fairer distribution of public goods and social justice for the poor, ending corruption and upholding democracy (Naushin, 2006). Ironically, at the same time, some other civil society organisations in the country were also divided; aligning themselves either with the government or opposition camps. Civil society groups that were aligned with the opposition had to accept the effects of governmental high-handedness; whereas, on the other hand, other civil society organisations benefitted from the patronage of the ruling political party (Huq, 2005).

Today, Bangladeshi civil society can be categorised into different segments, such as, intellectuals, academicians, NGOs, corporate groups and owners of print and electronic media. The strongest segment is composed of the intellectuals and academicians. They dominate Blogs, Facebook, print media and TV talk shows, as they express their views. However, they are strongly divided by factional, political ideologies, which has weakened their ability to represent the mass public (Lewis, 2011). NGOs, on the other hand, influence a larger portion of Bangladeshi society by directly getting involved with citizen rights and social benefits such as health care, social welfare, education and safety net packages. Among thousands of others, Bangladesh Rural Advancement Committee (BRAC), Proshika, Grameen Bank, Nijera Kori, Association for Social Advancement (ASA) have set examples of how to achieve positive changes at the grassroots level in the areas of child and maternal health, gender rights, education, environmental protection, women's empowerment and the rights of the child (Yunus, 1999; Khandker, 1999; Sarker, Salam and Islam, 2012; Blair, 2005; Chaney, 2017). Print and electronic media have also been very instrumental in strengthening civil society in Bangladesh by standing against the coerciveness of the state. There are, however, counter-accusations that political elites also own electronic media to propagate their ideology (White, 1999).

It should also be noted that there are different forms, ideologies and practices within civil society in Bangladesh. On the one hand, there are conservative groups consisting of businessmen, political party members, religious and social advocates (Maclean, Quadir, & Shaw, 1997). On the other hand, as noted, progressive civil society groups are mostly dominated by intellectuals, academicians, lawyers, doctors, students, women, environmental activists and NGOs (Quadir, 2003). Rural-based civil societies are mostly focused on local advocacy activities and comprise a collective of co-operatives. In contrast, progressive civil society groups, which are mostly urban-based, tend to focus on development, democratic and rights-based activities by upholding welfare and redistributive philosophies. Thus, the contemporary form and functioning of civil society in Bangladesh is complex and dynamic. In the following sections, we consider its origins with reference to successive periods, beginning with the 1970s.

State, NGOs and Civil Society in Bangladesh: The Collaboration in the 1970s

The earliest formal NGOs and civil society organisations in Bangladesh can be traced back to the 1970s. Their existence stemmed from the call by the state to collaborate in promoting development for the newly independent Bangladesh. It became almost impossible for the government of Bangladesh to alone promote development and overall public service provisions due to devastating nine-month long independence war in 1971. This compelled the state to seek support from national and international organisations. In turn, this opened up an opportunity for civil society organisations to be directly involved in various development activities, such as poverty reduction through the provision of microcredit, education, environmental protection and local infrastructure development. Three factors facilitated the burgeoning of civil society organisations in Bangladesh at this time. First, the long-standing local culture of voluntarism and cooperation. This was initially set back by the call-to-arms in the nine-month long liberation war in 1971 and natural disasters that subsequently shattered the economy and infrastructure of the country. It was reinstated by the NGOs in the form of group or *samiti*[3] (Salehin, 2016). Second, civil society was bolstered by the call of the Government of Bangladesh to national and international organisations to help and support rebuilding the war-damaged nation. It was also facilitated by the availability of a vast amount of foreign aid that helped NGOs in Bangladesh flourish. Third, as a catalyst to development and the rise of civil society, most of the donor organisations such as World Bank, UNDP, DFID preferred to work with NGOs, which, in contrast to politically comprised state agencies, were believed to be less corrupt, non-bureaucratic, flexible and capable of reaching people who live in poverty-ridden and hard-to-reach rural areas. This, as well as adoption of neoliberal market economic reforms by the state, led to the burgeoning of civil society organisations (Haque, Das and Rahman, 2017).

Using the spirit of voluntarism, during the 1970s, most of the NGOs started working with communities and brought significant changes in different areas of development such as education, health, gender rights, women's empowerment and poverty reduction. While many local and national organisations were being established in rural and urban areas, they started to maintain a vertical relationship with external donor agencies (Rahman, 2019). Although the exact number of NGOs and civil society organisations is unavailable, it is believed that more than 22,000 NGOs are currently operating in Bangladesh. Among these, some are big and influential such as BRAC, Grameen Bank, Proshika, ASA, whereas, others are small establishments in the rural areas but equally contributing to the overall promotion of development (Mollah et al., 2019). The government realised the need for civil society organisations or, more specifically NGOs, because they could reach those places where the state is unable to due to various constraints, including financial and manpower shortages. Larger NGOs such as BRAC, Grameen Bank, Proshika and ASA received significant funding from the international donors and took part in welfare and development activities such as education, poverty reduction, health, hygiene and family-planning services. At this time, many other local and small NGOs also benefitted from the global funding and got directly involved in providing basic services to the poor (Davis and McGregor, 2000).

The collaboration[4] phase between the state and NGOs in the 1970s had been facilitated by the support of the government on the one hand and aid from donors on the other. The state needed support from the NGOs to implement many of the development programmes that were supported by donors. The need to rebuild the nation brought both the state and NGOs closer to each other. NGOs worked as a partner of the state in delivering services to the people. Both NGOs and the state found it mutually advantageous to work together for at least two reasons—first, the NGOs found it useful for legitimising the use of donor funds and an opportunity to work for the poor and rebuilding the nation. From a crudely nationalistic sense, working with the state also provided a sense of fulfilment for the NGOs. On the other hand, the state found it helpful to continue her service deliveries to the people with the support of the NGOs, which it otherwise found difficult because of its limited capability both in terms of manpower and the inability to reach all citizens. White succinctly points this out:

> For the NGOs, working with the state offers an opportunity to expand the scope of their operations, broaden their influence and participate in the formulation of the national development agenda. The state, on the other hand, may see collaborating with the NGOs as a chance to gain some reflected moral glory, retrieve a hold on donor funds, neutralize potential opposition, and achieve more efficient and cost-effective implementation of policy. (White, 1999)

The State, NGOs and Civil Society during the Military Regime in the 1980s

With the assassination of Bangabandhu Sheikh Mujibur Rahman in 1975, a military regime was initiated in Bangladesh with Major General Ziaur Rahman coming to power followed by General Hussain Muhammad Ershad that continued until 1990. Over the 15 years of authoritarian military regimes, both military authority and civil society organisations mutually benefitted from each other. The military authority had gained from civil society organisations by ensuring popular support, which was mobilised by the civil society organisations. The military state had also reinforced its hegemony by co-opting intellectuals and academics by rewarding them with top positions in the bureaucracy or public services. Many civil society organisations, by maintaining good relationship with the military government, won state support and funding (Tasnim, 2017; Quadir, 2003, 2015; Jamil, 1998). The military regime also consolidated power by maintaining either 'civil-military consensus' or 'carrot-stick' policies. Those who accepted military authority received state patronage; whereas, dissidents were harshly treated (Alam, 1995). To further consolidate their grip on power, both General Ershad and his predecessor General Zia adopted strict state controls on the media.

Both Generals created a support base through military and civil clientelism. The enormous flow of foreign aid was distributed among the loyal civil society organisations to win their support.

However, repressive measures were also taken by reshaping school textbooks, curbing political activities, maintaining alliances with powerful families, military officials and corporate groups (Codron, 2007). Immediately after coming to power Hussain Muhammad Ershad declared Martial Law to curb any sort of dissidence from the civil and political organisations. However, one of the first direct conflicts that emerged was that against Ershad's controversial educational policy, which was to Islamicise the secular educational system of Bangladesh by introducing the learning of Arabic as a mandatory language at primary school level, which the intellectuals and university students immediately rejected. A nationwide student strike was severely repressed by the military with the killing of a number of student protestors (Uddin, 2006). As a repercussion, any kind of association and freedom of labour unions had been restricted with the implementation of privatisation of many financial and industrial institutions. The military regime did not only continue to systematically influence politics of Bangladesh but also institutionalised military control in the civilian administration by introducing a quota-system for military officials in different civilian positions (Wolf, 2013). Three particular strategies had been followed by General Ershad to take control over civil societies in Bangladesh, which Huq succinctly points out as:

> The Ershad government adopted a three-fold strategy to exercise control and restrain civil society's onslaught. In doing so, it sought to crush the kernel of opposition inherent in the country's literacy and cultural traditions, which were a source of values and ethics. First, Ershad won over some intellectuals by means of inducements. Second, he tried to improve State control over diverse cultural activities. Third, he wanted to liquidate the authentic cultural tradition of the people of Bangladesh. (Huq, 2005)

Despite all these initiatives to consolidate power, the Generals could not survive. The most powerful dissent came from intellectuals, artists, student unions and progressive civil society organisations who raised their voice, mobilised the people and protested against the regime. It was mostly because of the active role of the civil society organisations that the military regime was challenged and eventually overthrown in 1990 (Rizvi, 1991). The military regime could thus be characterised as having employed both repressive as well as patronising measures to control civil society organisations. Civil society organisations responded by either aligning with the regime to receive state benefits; or, in the case of liberal and pro-democratic organisations, stood against the regime and played a significant role to eventually overthrow it.

State, NGOs and Civil Society in the 1990s: Corporatisation and Confrontation

With the fall of the military regime, the return to election and parliamentary democracy in 1990 signalled that democratic governance in Bangladesh would prevail. However, soon after the election, that dream turned into despair as political clashes, violence and strikes started between the ruling party and the opposition on accusations of corruption, political revenge and monopoly of the state power by the ruling party (Hossain, 2000; Jahan, 2005). Rather than promoting democracy and good governance, a patron-client based political culture evolved over the time to replace the earlier political co-option. Civil society organisations were no exception and their relationship with the state had turned out to be one of dependence. Democratic institutions were still predominantly politicised along party lines and were not completely independent of state control, and thus, these institutions served the interests of the parties more than the citizens, as Farhat explains:

> Such relationships bring CSOs favors for the group, such as project sanctions, financial grants, and jobs, as well as personal favors, including government loans, employment, promotions, business

> grants and licenses, government contracts, legal aid, and even medical help. In return, the government and political parties receive loyalty and support from different sections of the social strata, financial and logistic support during elections, control over different institutions and even the media, and ensure the necessary organisational base for staging mass protests. (Tasnim, 2017)

While working on such issues as demanding public entitlements, women's empowerment, gender rights, distribution of tax-free lands (*khas* lands) to the poor, and poverty alleviation programmes, many civil society organisations came into conflict with the powerful interest groups and local elites, mostly supported by the ruling political parties who occupied the top positions in government and society and controlled state resources. Two consequences became particularly evident due to the mass-mobilisation of NGOs: millions of poor people demanded their rightful public entitlements (such as state tax-free lands or gender rights); and, NGOs achieved a kind of power, which Huque (2005) refers to as the emergence of a 'shadow state'. Rightly, the state authorities feared mobilisation of the poor. Their fears were well-founded in the case of Proshika when it mobilised thousands of its microcredit borrowers to topple the Khaleda Zia government in 2004 and 2006 (see Chowdhury, 2001; Seabrook, 2004; Lewis 2017). A further prominent tension of the time was that between the state and Muhammad Yunus of Grameen Bank. It was triggered by Yunus's expression of interest to run in the national elections and form a political party called Nagorik Shakti[5] (Reuters, 2007). The matter went to court when ruling Awami League government sought to change the governance structure of the Bank and formed the Grameen Bank commission to strengthen the state's control of and influence over Grameen Bank (*The Guardian*, 2012). Hashemi has rightly observed such confrontation between the NGOs and the state:

> When the poor are organised to articulate their demands, to fight for their rights, and to struggle for changing the structural basis of their

> subordination, it most definitely implies challenging the status-quo. When governmental agencies perceive of their responsibilities as that of maintaining 'law and order' of the prevailing status-quo, it clearly sees the NGO activity as being threatening. (Hashemi, 1993)

State suppression of NGOs and legal measures to control those organisations that the government believes are political has seen NGOs switch to non-political modes of operation. This has largely depoliticised the development and civil society in Bangladesh. The formation of the NGO Affairs Bureau (1990), the issuing of a Circular on Working Procedures for Foreign and Foreign Assisted Bangladeshi Non-Governmental Organisations (NGOs) Working in Bangladesh (2012), and the enactment of the Foreign Donation Act (2016) are some of the steps taken by the state to register and regulate NGO activates. The NGO Affairs Bureau has the authority to grant or deny official approval of NGOs' receipt of foreign funds. This has given the NGO Affairs Bureau great powers that can be exercised in the narrow political interest of the state. It can, for example, determine which projects should and should not be funded. Something that should solely be the choice of the NGOs (Hashemi, 1993).

In this way, funding has become another important issue determining state–NGO relations. It carries the risk that, rather than being independent, NGOs become politically aligned with the government or foreign donors. Since most of the NGOs heavily depend on the funding sources either from the state or international donors, they have to try and maintain good relations with these stakeholders. Often this comes at a price as they compromise on their organisational aims and political values (see Tasnim, 2017; Hashemi, 1993; White, 1999; Haque, 2002).

All of this has opened up a new era in development practice in Bangladesh where most of the NGOs are either corporatised and/or forced to use microcredit schemes or social business to generate funds for their very survival (Lewis, 2016; Fernando and Devine, 2003). Others have developed business strategies to market their goods and services to the target groups. For example, BRAC started its first retail cottage store *Aarong* in 1978, while Grameen Bank, ASA, *Thengamara Mohila Sabuj Sangha* (TMSS) all started commercial ventures in many sectors, including: dairy farming, telecommunications, universities, hospitals and medical colleges (Chowdhury, 2017; Chowdhury and Willmott, 2018). Such a proliferation of commercial ventures has been possible due to the strategic use of the accumulated profit of the NGOs from their microcredit programme as well as the Bangladesh government's neoliberal market policy of privatising most of its services. Many NGOs have taken this opportunity to expand their commercial ventures. In consequence, they have moved away from their earlier objectives and the political mobilisation of the 1970s, which was mostly focused on relief, rehabilitation and welfare activities. Instead, today NGOs now appear to be corporatised and have become an indispensable part of the market economy. Although this has opened up an opportunity for the NGOs to ensure financial sustainability, critics argue it has come at a great cost for organisational sustainability has taken precedence over the interests of the poor (Fernando and Devine, 2003).

Conclusion: The Trajectories of an Uneasy Relationship between the State and Civil Society

As the foregoing discussion reveals, the state, NGOs and civil society organisations in Bangladesh have gone through various phases of interaction. Although different charitable organisations, religious and other welfare initiatives preceded the contemporary form of NGOs and civil society, the institutionalisation of NGOs supported by international donor funding dates back to the 1970s when, with the call for assistance from the newly formed Government of Bangladesh, they became directly involved with relief and rehabilitation programmes to rebuild war-damaged Bangladesh. This initial phase of interaction can be identified as enthusiastic cooperation and collaboration among the state, NGOs and other civil society organisations, which worked hand-in-hand for the practical purpose of rebuilding the nation. The major financial and moral support from the donor organisations facilitated the burgeoning role of NGOs during this time. However, facing a financial crisis, the newly formed government failed to deliver much-needed public services. Instead it turned to civil society. As the state struggled it was NGOs and civil society organisations that provided services for the mass of people.

With the assassination of Bangabandhu Sheikh Mujibur Rahman and the subsequent military coup d'état, the state of Bangladesh lost its democratic governance for the next 15 years (1975–1990). Initially, the military regime welcomed the existence of NGOs and civil society organisations to legitimise and consolidate its grip on power. Very soon, however, the Generals revealed their true autocratic nature and imposed strict regulations and control over media and suppressed civil society organisations. In short, 'carrot and stick' policies were adopted to deal with civil society organisations. Some aligned with the military regime and were patronised by the state; while many others vehemently opposed the regime. Some NGOs were under secret surveillance to monitor their anti-military state activities. The formation of Foreign Donation Regulation Act in 1978 and, subsequently, the creation of the NGO Affairs Bureau in 1990 were the first steps to control NGOs through oppressive registration and financial regulation. Many civil society organisations feared that the Bureau might be used as a means to extend further the coercive authority of the state. In response, liberal and pro-democratic civil society organisations helped oust the military regime.

With the return to democracy in the 1990s, it was expected that an auspicious environment would return for NGOs and civil society organisations. However, the clash between the political parties soon severely affected and halted the democratic process in Bangladesh. The political backlash almost paralysed the everyday life of the Bangladeshis with major consequences for state–NGO–civil society relations. For the first time in Bangladesh, some NGOs were seen to be directly aligned with political parties. Proshika had been in the forefront to mobilise its microcredit borrowers to topple down the government. The government immediately reacted by arresting hundreds of Proshika employees who were then convicted of involvement in anti-state activities. The state–NGO relationship further deteriorated when Muhammad Yunus, the founder of Grammen Bank, expressed his desire to form Nagarik Shakti as a political party to run in elections. The state feared that the mass mobilisation of Grameen microcredit borrowers might challenge its authority. This immediately led to repressive actions against Grameen Bank. This period can be characterised as one in which the state sought to make sure that the NGOs fully complied with its rules and regulations. NGOs, on the other hand, pressed to be freed from state coercion to fully achieve their development goals. This has led to an uneasy relationship between the state and the civil society.

More recently, a shortage of foreign funding has added another dimension of state–NGO relationship. It has meant that many NGOs have been forced to focus on their own sustainability as an organisation. As a consequence, NGOs have now been corporatised as they operate microcredit schemes or venture into business activities such as establishing medical colleges, telecommunications, universities, dairy farms and the sale and marketing of handicrafts. Moving away from their original objectives as non-profit development organisations in the 1970s, many NGOs have now become part of the rise of the so-called 'social businesses' as invented by Muhammad Yunus. Such a transition from non-profit to profit motivation challenges and transforms the nature of NGOs and their relationship with the state. As the foregoing discussion has revealed, over the past half-century, state–NGO–civil society relations have gone through various phases: cooperation and collaboration in the 1970s, followed by suppression during the military regime in the 1980s and a rather uneasy relationship in the 1990s due to NGOs being drawn into party politics. This history underlines that whilst some theorisations view NGOs and civil society organisations as independent of the state, market and politics, the Bangladeshi experience shows how they are being co-opted, suppressed and intimately involved in politics and business matters.

Notes

1. 'Palli Mangal Samiti' can roughly be translated as rural welfare society, which has its history dated back to the colonial period initiated mostly by the rural benevolent landlords to support welfare activities of the rural farmers.
2. These are all series of movements by the East Pakistani people against the oppression of the then West Pakistani government against imposing languages, demands of autonomy and fight for independence.
3. *Samiti*, a Bengali word which literally refers to a group of people, has become a household word in Bangladesh precisely because of its usage by the NGOs. *Samiti*, a group of usually 10–15 people, is formed in the community by the NGOs as a platform to deliver their services.
4. For more detail on collaboration and complementarities among the civil society organisations, see Wessel, Naz and Sahoo (2020).
5. During the interim caretaker government in between 2006 and 2008, when most of the top politicians were imprisoned in charge of corruption and a state of emergency existed, Dr Muhammad Yunus, Noble Laureate and founder of Grameen Bank, expressed his intentions to run into election by forming a political party called Nagorik Shakti or Citizen's Power. Many believed that the base of power of his intention were the millions of microcredit borrowers of Grameen Bank. Yunus finally gave up his intention.

References

Abed, F.H. and A.M.R. Chowdhury. 1997. 'The Bangladesh Rural Advancement Committee: How BRAC Learned to Meet Rural People's Needs through Local Action'. In *Reasons for Hope: Instructive Experiences in Rural Development*, edited by A. Krishna, 41–56, Connecticut: Kumarian Press.

Adamson, W. 1980. *Hegemony and Revolution: A Study of Antonio Gramsci's Political and Cultural Theory*. Berkeley: University of California Press.

Ahmed, M.M. 2003. 'Distant Voices: The Views of the Field Workers of NGOs in Bangladesh on Microcredit'. *The Geographical Journal*, 169(1): 23–39.

Alam, S.M.S. 1995. 'Democratic Politics and the Fall of the Military Regime in Bangladesh'. *Bulletin of Concerned Asian Scholars*, 27(3): 28–42.

Anderson, P. 1976. 'The Antinomies of Antonio Gramsci'. *New Left Review*, 100: 5–78.

Arato, A. 1989. 'Civil Society, History and Socialism: Reply to John Keane'. *Praxis International*, 9(1+2): 133–151.

Blair, H. 2005. 'Civil Society and Pro-poor Initiatives in Rural Bangladesh: Finding a Workable Strategy'. *World Development*, 33(6): 921–936.

Chandhoke, N. 1995. *State and Civil Society: Explorations in Political Theory*. New Delhi: Sage Publications.

Chaney, P. 2017. 'Limited Gains, Enduring Violations: Civil Society Perspectives on the Implementation of the United Nations' Convention on the Rights of the Child in Bangladesh'. *Journal of South Asian Development*, 12(3): 286–307.

Chowdhury, A. 2001. 'Local Heroes'. *New Internationalist*, 332: 22–24.

Chowdhury, R. and H. Willmott. 2018. 'Microcredit, the Corporatization of Nongovernmental Organizations, and Academic Activism: The Example of Professor Anu Muhammad'. *Organisation*, 26(1): 122–140.

Chowdhury, R. 2017. 'The Rana Plaza Disaster and the Complicit Behavior of Elite NGOs'. *Organisation*, 24(6): 938–949.

Codron, J. 2007. 'Putting Factions "Back in" the Civil-Military Relations Equation Genesis, Maturation and Distortion of the Bangladeshi Army'. *South Asia Multidisciplinary Academic Journal.* Free standing Article. Available at https://doi.org/10.4000/samaj.230 (accessed on 23 August 2020).

Comaroff, J.L. and J. Comaroff. 1999. 'Introduction'. In *Civil Society and the Political Imagination in Africa*, edited by J.L. Comaroff and J. Comaroff, 1–43. Chicago: The University of Chicago Press.

Davis, P.R. and J.A. McGregor. 2000. 'Civil Society, International Donors and Poverty in Bangladesh'. *Journal of Commonwealth & Comparative Politics*, 38(1): 47–64.

DeWiel, B. 1997. 'A Conceptual History of Civil Society: From Greek Beginnings to the End of Marx'. *Past Imperfect*, 6: 3–42.

Diamond, L. 1999. *Developing Democracy: Towards Consolidation*. Baltimore: John Hopkins University Press.

Fernando, J.L. and J. Devine. 2003. 'The Paradox of Sustainability: Reflections on NGOs in Bangladesh'. *Annals of the American Academy of Political and Social Science,* 590(2): 227-242.

Fisher, J. 1998. *Non-Governments: NGOs and the Political Development of the Third World*. West Hartford: Kumarian Press.

Fukuyama, F. 1995. *Trust: The Social Virtues and the Creation of Prosperity*. New York: The Free Press.

Gellner, E. 1994. *Conditions of Liberty: Civil Society and Its Rivals*. London: Hamish Hamilton.

Grimsley, R. 1973. *The Philosophy of Rousseau*. Bungay, Suffolk: Oxford University Press.

Hamilton, C.H. 1994. 'The Ties That Bind'. *The American Scholar*, 63: 140–42.

Haque, A.C., A. Das and A. Rahman. 2017. 'The Effectiveness of Micro-credit Programmes Focusing on Household Income, Expenditure and Savings: Evidence from Bangladesh'. *Journal of Competitiveness*, 9(2): 17–29.

Haque, M.S. 2002. 'The Changing Balance of Power between the Government and NGOs in Bangladesh'. *International Political Science Review*, 23(4): 411–435.

Hashemi, S.M. 1993. *Government and NGOs in Bangladesh: Coexistence, confrontation and collaboration*. Dhaka: CDL.

Hossain, A. 2000. 'Anatomy of Hartal Politics in Bangladesh'. *Asian Survey,* 40(3): 508–529.

Howell, J. and J. Pearce. 2002. *Civil Society and Development: A Critical Exploration*. Boulder: Lynne Rienner.

Hulme, D. and M. Edwards. 1997. *NGOs, States and Donors: Too Close for Comfort?*. London: Macmillan.

Huque, P.A. 2005. 'Civil Society and Democracy in Bangladesh'. *Social Change*, 35(2): 85–100.

Hyden, G. 1997. 'Civil Society, Social Capital, and Development: Dissection of a Complex Discourse'. *Studies in Comparative International Development*, 32(1): 3–30.

Islam, M.S. 2015. *Pursuing Alternative Development: Indigenous People, Ethnic Organisation and Agency*. London: Palgrave Macmillan.

_______. 2004. 'Who Benefits, How Benefits: The Political Economy of Grameen Bank's Microcredit Programme in Rural Bangladesh'. *South Asian Anthropologists*, 4(1): 1–12.

Jahan, R. 2005. *Bangladesh Politics: Problems and Issues*. Dhaka: The University Press Limited.

Jamil, I. 1998. 'Transactional Friction between NGOs and Public Agencies in Bangladesh: Culture or Dependency?'. *Contemporary South Asia*, 7(1): 43–70.

Keane, J. 1988. *Civil Society and the State: New European Perspectives*. London: Verso books.

Khandker, S.R. 1999. *Fighting Poverty with Microcredit: Experience in Bangladesh*. Dhaka: The University Press Limited.

Klein, S. and C.S. Lee. 2019. 'Towards a Dynamic Theory of Civil Society: The Politics of Forward and Backward Infiltration'. *Sociological Theory*, 37(1): 62–88.

Kumar, K. 1993. 'Civil Society: An Enquiry into the Usefulness of an Historical Term'. *British Journal of Sociology*, 44(3): 375–395.

Kwon, H.K. 2004. 'Associations, Civic Norms, and Democracy: Revisiting the Italian Case'. *Theory and Society*, 33(2): 135–166.

Lewis, D. 2004. 'On the Difficulty of Studying Civil Society: Reflections on NGOs, State and Democracy in Bangladesh'. *Contributions to Indian Sociology*, 38(3): 300–322.

_______. 2011. *Bangladesh: Politics, Economy and Civil Society*. Cambridge: Cambridge University Press.

_______. 2016. 'Non-Governmental Organisations and Civil Society'. In *Routledge Handbook of Contemporary Bangladesh*, edited by A. Riaz and M.S. Rahman, 119–128, London and New York: Routledge.

_______. 2017. 'Organising and Representing the Poor in a Clientelistic Democracy: The Decline of Radical NGOs in Bangladesh'. *The Journal of Development Studies*, 53(10): 1545–1567.

Lovell, C.H. 1992. *Breaking the Cycle of Poverty: The BRAC Strategy*. Connecticut: Kumarian Press.

Maclean, S.J., F. Quadir and T.M. Shaw. 1997. 'Structural Adjustment and the Response of Civil Society in Bangladesh and Zimbabwe: A Comparative Analysis'. *New Political Economy*, 2(1): 149–164.

Mollah, T.H., S. Shishir, W. Ullah and T. Nihei. 2019. 'Assessing NGOs Micro-credit Programs: A Geo-spatial and Socio-economic Scenario from Rural Bangladesh'. *International Review of Economics*, 66(2): 79–99.

Naushin, P.S. 2006. 'Civil Society and Good Governance in Bangladesh'. *Asian Journal of Political Science*, 14(2): 189–211.

Neocleous, M. 1995. 'From Civil Society to the Social'. *The British Journal of Sociology*, 46(3): 395–408.

Putnam, R. 1993. *Making Democracy Work: Civic Traditions in Modern Italy*. Princeton: Princeton University Press.

Quadir, F. 2003. 'How "Civil" is Civil Society? Authoritarian State, Partisan Civil Society, and the Struggle for Democratic Development in Bangladesh'. *Canadian Journal of Development Studies*, 24(3): 425–438.

_______. 2015. 'Civil Society in Bangladesh: In Search of Democracy and Development'. In *Civil Society in Asia: In Search of Development and Democracy in Bangladesh*, edited by F. Quadir and Y. Tsujinaka, 1–18, Farnham: Ashgate.

Rahman, A. 2019. *Women and Microcredit in Rural Bangladesh: An Anthropological Study of Grameen Bank Lending*. London and New York: Routledge.

Reuters. 2007. 'Bangladesh Nobel Winner Names New Political Party'. *Reuters*. London, 18 February.

Rizvi, G. 1991. 'Bangladesh: Towards Civil Society'. *The World Today*, 47(8/9): 155–160.

Sahoo, S. 2013. *Civil Society and Democratization in India*. London and New York: Routledge.

_______. 2014. 'Civil Society and Democratization: A Counter-case from India'. *Democratization*, 21(3): 480–500.

Salehin, M.M. 2016. *Islamic NGOs in Bangladesh: Development, Piety and Neoliberal Governmentality*. London and New York: Routledge.

Sarker, M.F.H., M.A. Salam and M.S. Islam. 2012. 'Does Microcredit Help Promote Development and Peace at the Household Level in Bangladesh?'. *Research Journal of Social Science and Management*, 2(2): 14–19.

Seabrook, J. 2004. 'In the Shadow of the Torture'. *New Internationalist*, Oxford, 2 August.

Tasnim, F. 2017. 'Politicized Civil Society in Bangladesh: Case Study Analyses'. *Cosmopolitan Civil Societies: An Interdisciplinary Journal*, 9(1): 98–123.

Tester, K. 2014. *Civil Society*. London and New York: Routledge.

The Guardian. 2012. 'Muhammad Yunus and Bangladesh Government Battle Over Grameen Bank'. *The Guardian*, London, 21 November.

Uddin, A.K.M.J. 2006. 'The Movement for the Restoration of Democracy in Bangladesh 1982–1990: A Study of Political Sociology'. Unpublished PhD Thesis: School of Sociology and Social Policy, The University of Leeds.

Van Wessel, M., F. Naz and S. Sahoo. 2020. 'Complementarities in CSO Collaborations: How Working with Diversity Produces Advantages'. *Voluntas*. Available at https://doi.org/10.1007/s11266-020-00227-4 (accessed on 10 July 2020).

White, S.C. 1999. 'NGOs, Civil society, and the State in Bangladesh: The Politics of Representing the Poor'. *Development and change*, 30(2): 307–326.

Whitehead, L. 1997. 'Bowling in the Bronx'. In *Civil Society: Democratic Perspectives*, edited by R. Fine and S. Rai, 94–114. London: Franc Cass.

Wolf, S.O. 2013. 'Civil-Military Relations and Democracy in Bangladesh'. Heidelberg: APSA. Available at 10.2139/ssrn.2773091 (accessed on 6 August 2020).

Yunus, M. 1999. *Banker to the Poor: Micro-lending and the Battle against World Poverty*. New York: Public Affairs.

Conclusions

Civil Society and Citizenship in South Asia: Contemporary Malaise, Future Prospects

Paul Chaney and Sarbeswar Sahoo

In this concluding chapter, we reflect on the significance of the empirical and theoretical analysis and address three questions, namely, in the case study countries—what does the present volume tell us about: (a) gender rights, (b) minority rights and (c) state–civil society relations? The chapter concludes by considering the implications of the current findings for the future of civil society and citizenship in India and Bangladesh.

Women's Movements and Gender-Inclusive Citizenship

According to Lister (2012),

> Women have been denied the full and effective title of citizen for much of history, ancient and modern. The twentieth-century mainstream theorization of citizenship has tended to ignore the ways in which women's gradual achievement of civil, political and social rights often followed a different pattern from men's.

For Lister (2003), the modern idea of citizenship has been 'inherently woman-unfriendly'; it is unable to 'give full recognition to the different and shifting identities that women simultaneously hold'. Typically, 'women have been faced with a choice between a universalistic claim based on the principles of their equality with men or a particularistic claim based on their difference from men'. Both approaches have made a rigid gendered separation between *public* and *private* spheres—while the public sphere is exalted as the sphere of universalism, justice and independence, the private sphere has been derided as the sphere of particularity, care and dependence. Given that women are often relegated to the latter, Lister has advocated a feminist approach to citizenship or 'woman-friendly citizenship' that not only gives primacy to women's *agency* but also 'reconstructs citizenship along pluralist and gender-inclusive lines'.

In turn, this raises the question—who can represent women and advocate for gender-inclusive citizenship rights? The chapters in this book engage with this issue and have followed a gender pluralist conception of citizenship (Siim, 2000). They show how women's organisations and movements have played a vital role, not just in strengthening women's agency but also in fighting for their rights and enhancing their participation in the public sphere. They have also contributed significantly to the nation-building process and advanced the agenda of gender-inclusivity and pursuit of a gender-just society. Despite this, the following discussion reveals how at times it is women's movement that has obstructed itself in achieving gender-inclusive citizenship rights. The major issue is the question of *representation*—whether women's movements truly and successfully *represent* women's issues (for more on representation by development organisations, see Katyaini, Van Wessel and Sahoo, 2021). As Chapters 1 and 2 demonstrate, women's movements do not necessarily always represent women's issues. This is because many women's movements are often preoccupied with the larger question of equality and justice but are detached from the everyday lived realities and problems of *local* women. Furthermore, many of these movements are also caught in-between the structural complexities of the 'political field' which often negatively impacts on their objective of advancing gender-inclusive citizenship.

In Chapter 1, B. Rajeshwari's analysis charts the emergence of local Muslim women's organisations and how they are principally concerned with representing Muslim women because many in the community felt that a pan-Indian women's movement was not equipped to deal with their issues and needs, notably on the issue of personal laws. More broadly, this underlines the failure of the women's movement in India to incorporate Muslim women within its larger narrative. Despite the emergence of Muslim women's organisations, government intransigence and failings in the interpretation of their demands and struggles has not meant that their women are closer to gender justice. The wider failure of the women's movement to span Hindu and Muslim (as well as other) faiths means that there remain unanswered questions related to women's agency and participation in extremist movements and advancing exclusionary practices, thereby, undermining intersectional ties. In a darkly paradoxical twist, Rajeshwari shows how this may be seen as leading to a resurgent patriarchy that on several occasions gets tacit support from women's organisations themselves.

The experience in Bangladesh resonates with the foregoing. It also points to the need for cognisance of intersectionality and diversity. Moreover, it shows how feminist mobilisation is best understood in the context of Bourdieu's 'political field' and how women's movements are embedded in coalitions initiated by diverse women's organisations and shaped by their interaction with other actors, including diverse civil society groups, donors, UN agencies, NGOs, political parties and the state. As in the Indian case (and events such as Muslim Personal Law and the Shah Bano trial), the analysis underlines the need for a temporal perspective and highlights the role of 'critical junctures'. It shows how a sequence of events, including shifting governance practices, has led to the rise of NGO-isation, 'administrative' feminist forces and the de-radicalisation of the women's movement.

Minority Rights and Competing Conceptions of Citizenship

As Will Kymlicka (1995) notes, in the era after the Second World War,

> Many liberals hoped that the new emphasis on 'human rights' would resolve minority conflicts. Rather than protecting vulnerable groups directly through special rights for the members of designated groups, cultural minorities would be protected indirectly, by guaranteeing basic civil and political rights to all regardless of group membership. Basic human rights such as freedom of speech, association and conscience, while attributed to individuals, are typically exercised in community with others and so provide protection for group life. Wherever these individual rights are firmly protected, liberals assumed, no further rights needed to be attributed to the members of specific ethnic or national minorities.

However, as the cases of Muslim minorities in India and Rohingya refugees in Bangladesh show, this was a false assumption.

As Chapter 1 shows, Muslims of India have historically remained marginalised and their loyalty to the Indian nation has been repeatedly questioned by religious conservatives. A wider, related issue that needs to be addressed is the extent to which inequality and discrimination is institutionally embedded in the modern state, as well as the degree to which today's domestic legal code is consistent with international treaty obligations and promotes equality for all citizens and proscribes violence, maladministration and oppression.

Similarly, in case of the Rohingyas, the Bangladeshi government has concentrated on providing transitory humanitarian relief. In essence, as Chaney's account in Chapter 3 reveals, the official response continues to be one of containment based on notions of difference rather than the extension of citizenship and long-term integration of refugees into Bangladeshi society. It is also the case that the Rohingya crisis cannot be divorced from the wider issue of religious extremism and instability in the region (Chaney and Sahoo, 2020). In part, this has shaped the Government of Bangladesh's response to the crisis. This is because a small minority of Rohingya refugees are involved with Islamic extremists and associated with militant groups (such as the Arakan Rohingya Islamic Front and Jamaat-e-Islami). All are active in the border area of Myanmar and Bangladesh.

Crucially, shifting social relations in India and the Rohingya crisis in Bangladesh bring to the fore a clash of competing conceptions of citizenship. In the case of Bangladesh, this involves the ruling elite's response to Rohingya demands to be recognised as (equal) citizens. Specifically, for some Islamic Rohingya refugees, this involves pressing for a new mode of citizenship that challenges the established geo-politics of the region: namely, membership of a separate Islamic state. Thus, in part, the Government of Bangladesh's failure to extend citizenship rights to the Rohingyas not only reflects its limited capacity to extend aid, it also stems from its fear of extremism and a repetition of the Rohingya's influx of Bangladesh in 1978 that destabilised the government. Moreover, the humanitarian crisis in the refugee camps around Cox's Bazaar is not only about statelessness and the denial of national, Bangladeshi citizenship; it is also about the violation of key aspects of welfare citizenship, including breaches of UN Conventions on combating disease and malnutrition as well as the right to adequate shelter, freedom from violence and persecution and access to education and health care.

State–Civil Society Relations and Governance Practices

As Antoine Buyse (2018) notes, 'In many countries civil society is under pressure. Collective citizens' efforts, especially when they have political salience, seem to be regarded with increasing suspicion and even to be actively countered' (see also Chaney, 2018a, 2018b).

The present volume shows how South Asia is no exception to this global trend. In the case of India, as Sahoo details in Chapter 4, the state has become increasingly inflexible. In order to enhance its own legitimacy, it has aligned itself to a group of organisations within civil society that advance its political projects. During recent years, a particular kind of civil society group has become ascendant. Specifically, the state is providing active political, economic and legal support to civil society organisations that support its political project. At the same time, it is actively monitoring and constraining the activities of other civil society groups that question the government and its policies.

In the case of Bangladesh, as Islam and Sarker reveal in Chapter 5, over the last 50 years, NGOs and civil society have gone through several transformations. Notably, NGOs in Bangladesh have shifted from rights activism and relief and rehabilitation service provision in the 1970s to acting as more corporate organisations since the 1990s. This reflects the changing relationship between state, civil society and international aid in Bangladesh. Such corporatisation of the NGO sector is a reflection of the policies of the World Bank, IMF and other international donor institutions which seek to roll back the state and promote NGOs that are believed to be flexible and less corrupt, and able to engender citizen trust. Furthermore, the implementation of free-market ideology through structural adjustment policies in Bangladesh has reinforced the NGO-isation of civil society and, over recent years, diminished rights advocacy and mobilisation.

In conceptual terms, this volume underlines the need to understand state–civil society relations and contemporary citizenship rights from a governance perspective. That is, a systematic view that is cognisant of the interaction between the personal and familial sphere, as well as relations between the state, civil society and the market (Bevir, 2013; Jessop, 2016). In sociological terms, this aligns with Ray's interpretation of Bourdieu's notion of the 'field' as 'a structured, unequal, and socially constructed environment within which organizations are embedded and to which organizations and activists constantly respond' (Ray, 1999; Bourdieu, 2002). As the earlier chapters show, feminist theory and social movement analysis also provide useful lenses and underline the importance of intersectionality and reflexivity. They also underline the contingent nature of civil society and citizenship practices and how rights are shaped by temporal shifts in politics and governance practices (see, for example, Chapters 4 and 5).

The analysis in this volume also supports the classical work of liberal theorists such as Hobbes, Locke and Rousseau, as well as later thinkers, including De Tocqueville, in underlining the key importance attached to civil society criticality in order to uphold democracy and human rights. Crucially, the earlier analysis also gives credence to neo-Marxist scholars like Gramsci, for the contemporary struggles in both India and Bangladesh, demonstrate how civil society is a pivotal site of hegemonic and counter-hegemonic struggle (Kumar, 1993). Notably in India, whilst extant work shows the benign impact of NGOs' co-working (Van Wessel, Naz and Sahoo, 2020), the mobilisation of and support for NGOs aligned to narrow group interests underlines the salience of earlier work emphasising that not all civil society mobilisation is a benign force for democracy and uphold citizenship rights (Sahoo, 2013, 2014). Viewed in Habermasian terms, analysis of contemporary practices in both countries reveals limited evidence of civil society operating as a 'public sphere' wherein private individuals transcend their ascribed identities and come together as a public and form an interactive body of citizens engaged in a rational critical discourse (Calhoun, 1992). Instead, we are witnessing what might more aptly be described as the colonisation of the lifeworld, or repurposing of associative life in civil society (Habermas, 1987). This is because 'the system'—in the form of government and international development agencies—is placing increasing emphasis on bureaucratisation, commodification and service delivery (as captured in the term NGO-isation); rather than unbridled, sometimes radical, civil society mobilisation to uphold citizens' freedoms and challenge state dominance.

Civil Society and Citizenship in South Asia: Future Prospects?

This volume underlines how the contemporary struggle for citizenship rights in India and Bangladesh is multifaceted and cross-cut with complex, iterative interactions between gender, faith and secularism. It can also be shaped by the clash of traditional values and the forces of modernity. As Turner (2017) notes, the latter include the rise of globalisation, consumerism and the negative effects of capitalism and neoliberalism, widening inequalities and exacerbating patterns and processes of exclusion. Furthermore, the accounts in this volume emphasise how the very notion of citizenship is contested in India and Bangladesh. Furthermore, it reveals how profound patterns and processes of exclusion, inequality and oppression are often, though by no means exclusively, grounded in gender and religious discrimination, and reinforced by authoritarian government. Against this troubling backdrop, the Office of the High Commissioner for Human Rights aptly captures the challenge facing citizenship in South Asia today:

> Throughout the region, the need for human rights advocacy and protection has continuously escalated. Civil and democratic space has been reduced in some countries; human rights defenders and media professionals have increasingly been targeted, and respect for and protection of the rights to freedom of expression and peaceful assembly have declined. In many countries, electoral processes have been accompanied by violence and restrictions of fundamental rights. There is widespread impunity for serious human rights violations including torture, disappearances, extrajudicial killings, and lack of access to justice. (OHCHR, 2019)

The findings in this volume also point to the need to move away from the 'soft' rights exhortations of governments. These are largely discursive, symbolic and rhetorical (Cole, 2009). Crucially, they lack justiciability. In order to address the rights violations identified in the earlier chapters, governments need to embrace 'hard' rights that are legally enshrined and enforceable (Trubek and Trubek, 2005) and offer redress to the violated. This can be done by better incorporating international treaty obligations into the domestic legal codes of India and Bangladesh, along with strengthening domestic equality and human rights commissions, and ending the persecution of human rights defenders.

However, the most crucial determinant of future citizenship rights in India and Bangladesh is the form and functioning of civil society. In this regard, the findings in this volume support earlier work (grounded in the classic work of Alexis de Tocqueville), that concludes that 'improvement in human rights is typically more likely the more democratic the country … [In short,] ratification [of human rights treaties] is more beneficial the stronger a country's civil society is' (Neumayer, 2005). However, formidable challenges lie ahead in this regard. Foremost is the need to overcome state oppression and maintain civil society activism in order to hold governments accountable for their actions, including their response to international and domestic citizenship obligations. Here, the current analysis points to the centrality of generativity in determining the future of citizenship rights in the region. Coined by Erikson (1974), this term denotes 'a concern for establishing and guiding the next generation'. The rise of NGO-isation, the shift from mobilisation to service delivery amongst civil society organisations, the spectre of 'administrative' feminist forces and the de-radicalisation of social movements combine to offer the prospect of a future loss of civil society criticality as the present generation becomes ever more distant from past episodes of democratising citizen protest. In this regard, civil society in India and Bangladesh would do well to learn the lessons of the past and present—in order to safeguard the future.

References

Bevir, M. 2013. *The Sage Handbook of Governance*. London: Sage Publications.

Bourdieu, P. 2002. *Distinction: A Social Critique of the Judgment of Taste*. London: Routledge.

Buyse, A. 2018. 'Squeezing Civic Space: Restrictions on Civil Society Organizations and the Linkages with Human Rights'. *International Journal of Human Rights*, 22(8): 72–91.

Calhoun, C. (ed.). 1992. *Habermas and the Public Sphere*. MIT Press.

Chaney, P. and S. Sahoo. 2020. 'Civil Society and the Contemporary Threat to Religious Freedom in Bangladesh'. *Journal of Civil Society*, 16(3): 191–215.

Chaney, P. 2019. 'India at the Crossroads? Civil Society, Human Rights and Religious Freedom: Critical Analysis of CSOs' Third Cycle Universal Periodic Review Discourse 2012–2017'. *International Journal of Human Rights*, 25(5): 33–49.

________. 2018a. 'Civil Society, Human Rights and Religious Freedom in the People's Republic of China: Analysis of CSOs' Universal Periodic Review Discourse'. *International Journal of Human Rights*, 22(4): 19–29.

________. 2018b. 'Civil Society, "Traditional Values" and LGBT Resistance to Heteronormative Rights Hegemony: Analysis of the UN Universal Periodic Review in the Russian Federation'. *Europe–Asia Studies*, 70(4): 638–665.

Cole, W. 2009. 'Hard and Soft Commitments to Human Rights Treaties, 1966–2001'. *Sociological Forum*, 24(3): 563–588.

Erikson, E.H. 1974. *Dimensions of a New Identity*. New York: Norton.

Habermas, Jürgen. 1987 [1981]. *Theory of Communicative Action, Volume Two: Lifeworld and System: A Critique of Functionalist Reason*, Translated by Thomas A. McCarthy. Boston, MA: Beacon Press.

Jessop, B. 2016. 'Territory, Politics, Governance and Multispatial Metagovernance'. *Territory, Politics, Governance*, 4(1): 8–32.

Katyaini, S., M. Van Wessel and S. Sahoo. 2021. 'Representation by Development Organisations: Evidence from India and Implications for Inclusive Development'. *Journal of Environment and Development* , 30(1): 98–123.

Kumar, K. 1993. 'Civil Society: An Inquiry into the Usefulness of an Historical Term'. *British Journal of Sociology*, 44(3): 375–395.

Kymlicka, W. 1995. *Multicultural Citizenship a Liberal Theory of Minority Rights*. New York: Oxford University Press.

Lewis, D. 2013. 'Civil Society and the Authoritarian State: Cooperation, Contestation and Discourse'. *Journal of Civil Society*, 9(3): 325–340.

Lister, R. 2003. *Citizenship: Feminist Perspectives.* New York: Palgrave MacMillan, p. 197.

_______. 2012 'Citizenship and Gender'. In *The Wiley-Blackwell Companion to Political Sociology*, edited by E. Amenta, K. Nash and A. Scott, 372–382, London: Blackwell.

Neumayer, E. 2005 'Do International Human Rights Treaties Improve Respect for Human Rights?'. *Journal of Conflict Resolution*, 49(6): 925–30.

Office of the High Commissioner for Human Rights (OHCHR). 2019. *United Nations Human Rights Report 2019*. Geneva: United Nations Publication.

Ray, R. 1999. *Fields of Protest: Women's Movements in India*. Minnesota: University of Minnesota Press.

Sahoo, S. 2013. *Civil Society and Democratization in India: Institutions, Ideologies and Interests*. London: Routledge.

_______. 2014. 'Civil Society and Democratisation: A Counter-Case from India'. *Democratization*, 21(3): 480–500.

Sajó, A. and R. Uitz. 2017. *The Constitution of Freedom: An Introduction to Legal Constitutionalism*. Oxford: Oxford University Press.

Siim, B. 2000. *Gender and Citizenship*. Cambridge: Cambridge University Press.

Trubek, D.M. and L.G. Trubek. 2005. 'Hard and Soft Law in the Construction of Social Europe: The Role of the Open Method of Co-ordination'. *European Law Journal*, 11: 343–364.

Turner, B.S. 2017. 'Contemporary Citizenship: Four Types'. *Journal of Citizenship and Globalisation Studies*, 1(1): 10–23.

Van Wessel, M., F. Naz and S. Sahoo. 2020. 'Complementarities in CSO Collaborations: How Working with Diversity Produces Advantages'. *VOLUNTAS: International Journal of Voluntary and Non-Profit Organizations*, 5 May.

About the Editors and Contributors

Editors

Paul Chaney is Professor of Politics and Policy at Cardiff University, Wales, UK. He is the Co-Director of Wales Institute of Social, Economic Research and Data (WISERD). He has authored and edited 14 books and has written over 60 papers in international, peer-reviewed journals. His research and teaching interests include: territorial politics, public policy-making, civil society and equality and human rights.

Sarbeswar Sahoo teaches Sociology at the Indian Institute of Technology Delhi, India. He was Charles Wallace Fellow at Queen's University Belfast, UK, and Humboldt Postdoctoral Fellow at Max Weber Kolleg, University of Erfurt, Germany. He is the author of *Civil Society and Democratization in India* (2013) and *Pentecostalism and Politics of Conversion in India* (2018). He is also the co-editor (with Peter Berger) of *Godroads: Modalities of Conversion in India* (2020).

Contributors

Neera Chandhoke is a former Professor of Political Science at University of Delhi, India. She has published widely on civil society, secularism and minority rights. Her publications include: *Rethinking Pluralism, Secularism and Tolerance* (2019), *The Conceits of Civil Society* (2003), *Beyond Secularism* (1999), *State and Civil Society: Explorations in Political Theory* (1995) and others.

M. Saiful Islam is an anthropologist and an Associate Professor in the Department of Development Studies, University of Dhaka. He holds a PhD in anthropology from the National University of Singapore

(NUS) and an MPhil in anthropology from the Chinese University of Hong Kong. He is formerly the Programme Leader of Sociology and Anthropology at the University Brunei Darussalam. His research interests include sustainable development, medical anthropology, gender and migration issues. He is the author of *Culture, Health and Development in South Asia: Arsenic Poisoning in Bangladesh* (2017) and *Pursuing Alternative Development: Indigenous People, Ethnic Organization and Agency* (2015).

B. Rajeshwari is an Assistant Professor in the School of Humanities and Social Sciences, G.D. Goenka University, Sohna, Haryana. In 2019, she completed a collaborative post-doctoral fellowship with Indian Institute of Technology Delhi and the Wageningen University (Netherlands). Her research interests include gender studies, civil society, inter-religious conflict and post-conflict justice mechanisms. Her research papers have appeared in *World Development, Journal of Asian Security and International Affairs* and several other journals.

Seuty Sabur is Associate Professor of Anthropology in the Department of Economics and Social Sciences at BRAC University. She received her PhD from the National University of Singapore and MA from Hiroshima University, Japan. She has published in several international journals on gender and middle-class identity. One of her major publications is 'Marital Mobility in the Bangladeshi Middle Class' (*South Asia: Journal of South Asian Studies*, 2014).

Md Fouad Hossain Sarker is an Assistant Professor and Head of the Department of Development Studies at the Daffodil International University, Dhaka. His research interests include education and development, e-learning, gender, corporate social responsibility and e-governance.

Index